STEPPING
INTO
SCRIPTURE

D1227199

Liturgical Year B

May God bless you as the reading of his word

Shann Moore

Lillith O'Shann Edmiston Moore

ISBN 978-1-64670-077-6 (Paperback)
ISBN 978-1-64670-078-3 (Digital)

Covenant Books, Inc.
11661 Hwy 707
Murrells Inlet, SC 29576
www.covenantbooks.com

Contents

Foreword

Come along and join me in Stepping Into Scripture as we are taught God's word by his Holy Spirit. First pray then read the scripture a couple of times to grasp what is being said. Be patient and wait until you hear a word from the Lord. If other passages do not surface in your mind which provide more insight into the passage, look at cross reference scriptures. Once you hear what God is trying to teach you, outline the scripture passage into a flow chart. You now have a workable synopsis of the passage.

God's word is alive and active so you may not receive the same teaching I received. Just think of them as examples to help you develop a good study habit. Just let go with God and allow him to transform you through the reading of his word. New Revised Standard Version was used for scripture passages.

All of my thanks go to God. He blessed me with a passion for his word and he placed all of the people in my life who have encouraged this project. All I did was be obedient to the call. Thanks be to God.

STEPPING
INTO
ADVENT

	Advent 1 Year B 1 Corinthians 1:3–9 Partnership with God	
Trouble in River City Trouble in Corinth Paul writes letter to them and us	Through acts of piety and mercy, a partnership with God is formed.	This generous partnership with God has endless results (2 Corinthians 8:7).
Paul calls on grace and peace from God. Amazing grace and peace that we can't comprehend (Phil. 4:7).	Love God with all our heart, soul and strength and our neighbor as ourselves (Luke 10:27).	Endless faith—perpetual. Without faith it's impossible to please God for whoever comes to him must believe he exists (Heb. 11:6).
Paul gives thanks for God's grace, our enrichment in speech, knowledge, and every spiritual gift.	We love God through acts of piety. Some of these disciplines are praying, reading scripture, meditating, listening, and journaling.	Endless patience. Staying the course in our current situation knowing God works all things toward good (Rom. 8:28).
Thanks to God for strengthening us to the end so we will be blameless and for calling us into fellowship.	Love neighbor as ourselves by acts of mercy. Care for the sick, poor, homeless, visit the imprisoned, and make right any injustices.	Endless humility. Far beyond what we can see. "Humble yourself before the Lord, and he will exalt you" (James 4:10).
		God's grace upon grace enables us to do our part of this generous endeavor. God walks beside us and provides all we need (John 1:16).

Advent 1 Year B
Partnership with God
1 Corinthians 1:3–9

Just like River City, Paul sees trouble in Corinth, so he writes a letter. Paul writes this letter to the church of God in Corinth, to those sanctified in Christ Jesus, saints together with all those in every place who call on the name of the Lord Jesus Christ. This includes us.

Paul calls upon God's grace and gives thanks for all he has given us to enrich us and keep us blameless until the end. God calls us into an intimate fellowship and has equipped us with all we need to be in ministry with him.

Through acts of piety (a reverence for God expressed through spiritual disciplines), a fellowship is formed. These disciplines are how we love God with all our heart, soul, and strength.[1] Some of these disciplines include praying daily, reading scripture daily, meditating on what we have read, listening to what God has for us in his word and journaling. This takes time spent with the Lord, but we receive so much more back than we give.

Another way is through acts of mercy, loving your neighbor as yourself. Some of these acts are feed the hungry, give drink to the thirsty, clothe the naked, care for the homeless, visit the sick and those imprisoned, and look for injustices.

---

[1] Luke 10:27

Acts of piety and mercy bring us closer to God and the family of Christ. The results are the following:

- • Endless faith: perpetual, always there when we need it. Hebrews 11:6 reminds us that without faith it is impossible to please God. In this passage there is no mention of the size of our faith. It could be as small as a mustard seed.[2]
- • Endless patience: we stay the course in our current situation, knowing God works all things for good.[3] There is not a time element in the Roman passage so we have no idea when God will work, but we can be patient because we know he will work.
- • Endless humility: If we humble ourselves to the Lord, he will exalt us.[4] As the great theologian Mac Davis said, "O Lord it's hard to be humble." Being humble is hard for most of us because of that thing called pride. We may do good things, but generally, we want everyone to know we are good.

Our calling is to be in partnership with God through Christ Jesus. How that manifests itself will be different in each of our lives. But the end result is the same. We love God and neighbor, and God walks right along beside us in partnership. Through God's grace we are given grace upon grace[5] to enable us to do our part of the fellowship.

---

[2] Matthew 17:20
[3] Romans 8:28
[4] James 4:10
[5] John 1:16

Advent 2 Year B 2 Peter 3:8–15a Worth the Wait		
When we were kids we thought Christmas would never come. While we waited, we would wrap packages, send cards, visit family, and have big meals.	Chicago song: Does anybody really know what time it is? Does anybody really care?	While we wait we are to lead lives of holiness, set apart for God, to be in his likeness, his nature (Rom. 12:2).
We waited, anticipated, looked at the calendar, and marked off the days. We waited and waited and waited.	2 Peter is saying we don't know how much time until the Day of the Lord for it will come like a thief.	While we wait, lead lives of godliness; our inner response to the things of God. Develop the mind of Christ (Phil. 2:5). Practice spiritual disciplines.
We are now in a waiting season but we don't know the day and time, so no need to look at the calendar.	Like Christmas, we watch and wait. What type of lives should we be living while we wait? Faithful waiting includes holy conduct and godliness.	We are to be in the world but not part of it (John 17:16). Transformation of our minds and mind of others will change our world. It's up to us to start.
To God a day is like a thousand years. Psalm 90:4, a prayer of Moses. So we wait in hopeful expectation.		As we wait, we should strive to be found in peace, without spot or blemish (Phil. 2:14–15).
God is not slow as we think of slowness. He doesn't want anyone to perish (Hab. 2:3).		While we wait we should regard the patience of the Lord as salvation. He is waiting on those who do not know him. So it's worth the wait.
God's timing is not the same as ours. Chronos— our time, a specific time. Karios—God's time an opportune moment.		

Advent 2 Year B
Worth the Wait
2 Peter 3:8–15a

As a child, the hardest thing to do was wait for Christmas. We would look at the calendar as if that would hurry it right along. We would look at all the presents under the tree and wonder what was inside. While we waited, we made sure things were ready. We decorated a tree, sent Christmas cards, sang carols, and had family dinners. We waited and we waited and we waited. It seemed like forever.

We are now in a waiting season, but looking at a calendar won't help. We know God's timing is not the same as ours. We are on chronos, a specific time, and God is on kairos, an opportune moment. It's hard to imagine a thousand years being like a day to God. It is difficult for us to wrap our brain around it. So we wait in hopeful expectation. God is not slow as we think of slowness. He is patiently waiting on us to give up our will for his and have the same mind as Christ, a mind of one accord, one purpose, and unity with the Spirit.

Remember the song by Chicago that said, "Does anybody really know what time it is? Does anybody care? If so I can't imagine why. We've all got time enough to cry." Peter is trying to tell us we don't know if we have enough time or not since we do not know the day or the hour. Peter also says while we wait, there are certain things for us to do. Just like Christmas, while we wait, we need to make preparations for the day of the Lord.

While we wait we should lead a life of holiness. A life of holiness is a life set apart for God. It is the likeness of nature of God. We should not conform to this world but be transformed by the renewing of our minds so we can know the good, acceptable, and perfect will of God.[6]

While we wait we should live a life of godliness. Godliness in *Strong's Dictionary* is translated as piety, our inner response to the things of God. We should spend time with God in daily prayer, reading scriptures, meditating, listening, and journaling. This will help us develop the mind of Christ.[7]

While we wait we should strive to be found by him at peace without spot or blemish. "Do all things without murmuring and arguing so that you may be blameless and innocent children of God without blemish in the midst of a crooked and perverse generation, in which you shine like stars in the world".[8] Maybe we should think of ourselves as luminaries lighting the dark world.

While we wait we are to regard the patience of our Lord as salvation. The longer we wait there's a chance others will come to know God on a personal level. That makes it worth the wait.

---

[6] Romans 12:2
[7] Philippians 2:5
[8] Philippians 4:7

	Advent 3 Year B John 1:6–8, 19–28 The Voice of One	
It's difficult being a voice of one. John shows us how it can be done.	John had a clear understanding of who he was and who he wasn't. John understood his mission.	1. We need to know who we are and our individual ministry.
John aka the Baptizer was sent from God. In John's gospel, he never refers to him as the Baptizer because that was not his ministry.	Asked again who you are and what do you say about yourself, he answered them with OT scripture, Isaiah 40:3, declaring who he was.	2. We need to make straight the way of the Lord.
John's mission was to be a witness, to testify to the light that all might believe through him, the Messiah.	The Voice of One crying out in the wilderness; make straight the way of the Lord as the prophet Isaiah said.	3. We need to make straight the way of the Lord for others.
Questioned by the Jews and Levities sent by the Pharisee, he confessed he was not the Messiah, Elijah, nor the prophet (Deut. 18:15).	Greek transliteration for crying—to make an urgent distress call because an answer is needed.	4. We must give all credit and glory to God.
	Greek transliteration of make straight—to guide or steer. To do immediately without deviation or delay.	
	Greek transliteration of the way—journey, path, road.	

14

Advent 3 Year B
A Voice of One
John 1:6–8, 19–28

Have you ever been a voice of one; where you stood for the unconventional view? Did people laugh at you and call you names? It's not easy being a voice of one, but John shows us how it is done.

Right away scripture tells us about John who later was known as John the Baptizer. In John's gospel, he never revers to John as the Baptizer because that wasn't John's mission.

We learn John was a man sent by God to be a witness, to testify to the light so all might believe through him.

The Pharisees sent priests and Levites from Jerusalem who inquired of John, who was he? John confessed to them who he wasn't: the Messiah, Elijah, or the prophet. The prophet refers to Deuteronomy 8:15 where Moses says, "The Lord your God will raise up for you a prophet like me from among your own people; you shall heed such a prophet."

Probably John living in the wilderness reminded them of Moses leading them out of Egypt and the forty years spent in the wilderness.

Again these religious leaders asked "who are you," but this time they added a more specific question: "What do you say about yourself?" (Reminds me of the questions my parents would ask my dates.) Then John tells of his ministry because his mission was who he was. It was the reason he was born and gave meaning and purpose to his life. John quoted Isaiah 40:3 as his answer. He is the voice of one crying out in the wilderness, "Make straight the way of the Lord."

The Greek transliteration of cry means to make an urgent distress call when an answer is needed. The Greek transliteration of make straight means to guide or steer; to do immediately without deviation or delay. The Greek transliteration of way means journey, path, road. So John was issuing a distress call so he could guide others to the pathway leading to Jesus. This is also our ministry. Our ministries may not look the same but will be for a single purpose: introduce others to Jesus.

We need to make straight the way of the Lord. We need to remove any barriers or obstacles that keep us from running straight to Jesus with open arms. We need to make straight the way of the Lord for others.

We must give all credit and glory to God. We must know in our hearts and express with our mouths that we are not worthy to even stoop down and untie his sandals. Like John, we should put Jesus in the spotlight.

	Advent 4 Year B Luke 1:26–38 Let It Be	
Investigative reporter—Who: Mary, a virgin engaged to Joseph What: visited by the angel Gabriel	Do we have a questioning spirit? Do we ask twenty questions to determine all the details and what is in store for us?	Mary is given to us to be an example as to how we should answer God's call on our life.
When: sixth month Where: Nazareth of Galilee Why: to tell Mary she would be with child How: by the Holy Spirit	Do we have a doubting spirit? Do we tell God all the things we aren't able to do? Do we focus on our inability instead of God's ability?	Mary's spirit—humble, accepting, and trusting because she knew God would make a way for the impossible.
More investigation reveals Gabriel tells the name of the child and what he will be. Mary was perplexed, afraid, and questioned.	Do we have a complaining spirit? After we accept God's will, do we grumble and complain?	Serving spirit—Here am I, the servant of the Lord. Submitting spirit—Let it be.
Mary submitted, "Here am I, the servant of the Lord let it be with me according to your word."	Do we have a boasting spirit? Do we tell every one of our great sacrifice? Do we play the martyr? Does pride hinder our service?	When God calls, we must check to see what type of spirit. Hopefully he will find us accepting and trusting him to make the impossible happen.
True test of character is revealed by the way we deal with God's will for ourselves. Takes great character to submit to God's will.		May we think of the Beatles and say, "Let it be? Let it be. Dear Lord, let it be. Speaking words of wisdom, let it be."
Oswald Chambers said, "We all want to do God's will, we're just not sure how much it is going to hurt."		

Advent 4 Year B
Let It Be
Luke 1:26–38

Like a good investigative reporter, we need to ask some basic questions.

> Who: Mary, a virgin engaged to Joseph
> What: Visited by the angel Gabriel
> When: In the sixth month
> Where: Nazareth in Galilee
> Why: To tell Mary she would conceive a child
> How: By the Holy Spirit

We need to dig deeper for more information.

The sixth month refers to six months after Zechariah was told Elizabeth, though barren, would bear a son and they were to name him John. Zechariah questioned but scripture tells us he did not believe. So Gabriel made him mute and Zechariah invented charades and pictionary.

The angel Gabriel was once again sent on a mission, but this time to Mary who lived in Nazareth in Galilee. Luke 1:19 tells us that Gabriel stands in the presence of God. So we could say Gabriel is God's mouthpiece. And in Mary's song of praise, she describes herself as a lowly servant.

The first step to doing God's will is to believe it is God's will. The greatest test of character is revealed by the way we accept God's will. Oswald Chambers wrote, "We all want to do God's will. We're just not sure how much it is going to hurt." That pretty much sums it up, doesn't it? But God knows our hearts and our level of faith. He will call you to do something a little out of your comfort zone. When accomplished, your faith grows and you are stronger in your relationship with the Lord. Then he will call you to step out of your current comfort zone and again; once accomplished, your faith grows. God builds up our level of faith with every call to service.

When God calls us into ministry, however it may look, we need to think about these questions: Do we have a questioning spirit? Most times we ask twenty questions to see exactly what this mission will entail. Do we have a doubting spirit? Do we tell God all of the reasons we can't do it instead of focusing on God's ability to do the impossible? Do we have a complaining spirit? After we accept the call, like the Israelites, are we stiff-necked people who murmur and grumble about what we are asked to do? Do we have a boasting spirit? Do we go around telling people what God wants us to do and what a great sacrifice we are making? Do we allow pride to hinder our mission?

Mary was given to us an example of receiving God's will for our lives. When God calls, may we be found with a humble spirit, a servant spirit, and a submissive spirit.

When God calls, remember the Beatles and say, "Let it be, let it be, dear Lord let it be. Speaking words of wisdom, let it be."

	Christmas Eve/Day Year B Luke 2:1–20 Good News of Great Joy	
Shepherds lived in fields. Shepherds were held in low esteem because they had lived outside the polite society.	They went *now*.	The shepherds returned home glorifying and praising God.
In the still, an angel of the Lord appeared and told of the birth of Messiah and where the shepherds could find him.	Went without excuse or delay. Hear the urgency in *now*.	When God speaks to our spirit and we experience the wonders of the Lord, do we glorify and praise God?
What the shepherds did next was vital. Let us do likewise.	They went in haste. They didn't hesitate or linger. They were power walking.	When God speaks to our spirit and we experience amazing things, do we tell others and spread the word?
The shepherds knew the angel was from the Lord.	When God speaks to our spirit, do we go running to or running away from the Lord?	When God interrupts our plans and tells us to go in haste, we should put on our running shoes and *go*!
We must have a personal, intimate relationship with the Lord. We must be good spirit listeners.	The shepherds made known what had been told them about the child.	
When God speaks to our spirit, do we think about the inconvenience, how God interrupted our plans? We should just go.	When God speaks to our spirit, do we believe and tell others the amazing things we were shown.	

Christmas Eve/Day Year B
Good News of Great Joy
Luke 2:1–20

Let's put ourselves in the place of the shepherds to see how this might have played out.

We were sitting around the fire just like any other night. There did not appear to be anything out of the ordinary. The sheep had settled down for the night, so all was calm. The stars were shining in the sky although one did seem unusually bright. One of my fellow herdsmen pointed it out but we did not ponder it. Someone changed the subject and we were back to discussing the events of the day.

Suddenly there was a bright light and we were terrified. The vision spoke and told us not to be afraid. It was then we knew an angel of the Lord stood before us. The angel spoke of a child being born in the city of David and how we could find this child, who was Christ the Lord. Suddenly, in a blink of an eye, before us was a heavenly host praising God.

I turned to the other shepherds and told them we had to go and see the Christ child. We traveled by foot, hurried and quicken our pace as we were all eager to see the Child. And then we arrived at the stable and saw the baby lying in the manger. We found him wrapped in cloths just as the angel had said.

I still remember the smell of the sweet hay mingled with the stench of the animals. I remember how light it was compared to the darkness outside. I could tell there was something special about this child; the look on his face, the light shining on and around him.

I felt out of place as though I didn't belong. Of all the things in this scene, what didn't belong was this Child and his earthly parents. I, a shepherd, am used to the animals, and I carry their smell with me wherever I go. But this child, so holy, so innocent, should not be in this lowly place among such meager things.

All of us praised God for our Savior who was born this very night in the city of David. We rejoiced and told everyone we saw what had happened. Everyone was amazed. I was too for many reasons. I was amazed God would send angels to speak to shepherds, outcasts to most, to announce the birth of the Messiah. I was amazed that God had chosen me to be one of those to bear witness to this birth. I was amazed the Child was born in a stable, no home of his own. Yes, I was amazed. It was an amazing night. A holy night.

I'm sure Mary treasured all of these things in her heart and often thought about it. But so did I. I remember Mary sitting beside the manger watching the face of God's Child. What love she had on her face. But then she turned and said to me, "What is it you seek? What do you want?" This took me by surprise and caught me off guard. What did I want? Why was I there? But then I knew the only answer I could give, the only answer in my heart—I've come to worship.

STEPPING
INTO
CHRISTMAS

	Christmas 1 Year B Luke 2:22–40 The Law and the Holy Spirit Focus on v. 25–35	
Mary and Joseph obeyed God's will by observing Old Testament Law.	Simeon was a righteous and devout man.	Anna, a prophet, appeared at the temple "at just that moment." She too was righteous and devout. She came to worship, fast, and pray.
For Mary's purification they sacrificed a pair of turtledoves and two pigeons according to their means (Lev. 14:22).	The Holy Spirit rested on him because of his piety and devotion to God.	Interwoven throughout these scriptures are the presence and work of the Holy Spirit.
They presented Jesus in the temple to be named and circumcised as according to Law. Fourteenth chapter of Leviticus.	The Holy Spirit revealed to Simeon he would not taste death until he had seen the Lord's Messiah.	The Holy Spirit rests on those who are righteous and devout.
Old Testament Law required at least two witnesses. Enter Simeon and Anna.	The Holy Spirit guided him to the temple on that day: "…and the Lord whom you seek will suddenly come to his temple" (Mal. 3:1).	The Holy Spirit reveals to those who have open ears and open hearts (Isa. 30:21).

Christmas 1 Year B
The Law and the Spirit
Luke 2:21–40

Here we find Mary and Joseph obeying God's will through Old Testament Law. As required, Mary had presented herself for purification after she gave birth as found in the twelfth chapter of Leviticus. She and Joseph also offered a sacrifice of two turtledoves and two pigeons. According to the fourteenth chapter of Leviticus, this was the lowest level of payment and that each were to give as they could afford. We know Mary and Joseph were devout and righteous as they followed God's will as it was revealed to them. So if they gave turtledoves and pigeons as a sacrifice, we can be sure that was all they could afford. Mary and Joseph also followed God's will by presenting Jesus in the temple for naming and for circumcision. God instituted the rite of circumcision in seventeenth chapter of Genesis and the Law established in twelfth chapter of Leviticus.

In the Old Testament, to confirm a truth required two or three witnesses. Enter Simeon and Anna.

We are told Simeon was righteous and devout. They both were known as good and faithful servants of the Lord. Both of them affirmed Jesus as the Lord's Messiah, God's salvation and the redemption of Jerusalem.

The Holy Spirit rested on Simeon and he allowed the Spirit to reveal things and to guide him. The Spirit had revealed to Simeon that he would not taste death until he saw the Lord's Messiah. You might say this was the only thing on Simeon's bucket list. So he waited expectantly to see God's salvation. The Spirit led Simeon to the temple on the same day as the law required Mary and Joseph to present their baby in the temple. "…and the Lord whom you seek will suddenly come to his temple" (Mal. 3:1). As soon as Simeon saw the child, he began to prophesize. Using Old Testament language found in Isaiah chapters 40–66, Simeon testifies to the identity and the purpose of Jesus, the Lord's Messiah. He referred to him as God's salvation, a light for revelation to the Gentiles and for the glory of God's people, Israel. Gentiles and God's people, the chosen nation of Israel implies Jesus was the salvation for all people.

Simeon also predicted the future. He knew that the coming of redemption is also the advent of conflict. He professed that Israel would be divided as to Jesus's identity as the Lord's Messiah. And he told Mary a spear would pierce her heart, and it did.

Anna was a prophet, God's mouthpiece, and she also appears "at that moment" to worship in the temple. She also identified Jesus as the redemption of Israel. This was affirmation number 2 that Jesus was God's salvation, light, glory, and redemption for all.

Interwoven throughout this scripture is the presence and work of the Holy Spirit. The Holy Spirit rests on those who are righteous and devout. The Holy Spirit guides those who are attentive and have open ears and open hearts. The Holy Spirit helps us be obedient to God's will. "And when you turn to the right or when you turn to the left, your ears shall hear a word behind you, saying, This is the way, walk in it" (Isa. 30:21).

May the Holy Spirit rest on us all.

Watch Night/ New Year's Day Ecclesiastes 3:1–15 There Is a Time and a Season		
There is a season and a time for all things under heaven. By the time we get to time to die, we have experienced most of these seasons of time.	A time to weep and a time to laugh (Ps. 30:5b).	A time to tear and a time to sew (Joel 2:12–13).
God has placed a rhythmic order within us and within our world. But God determines the times.	A time to mourn and a time to dance (Ps. 30:11).	A time to keep silent and a time to speak (Ps. 39:2–3).
A time to be born and a time to die (John 12:24).	A time to throw away stones and a time to gather them together (John 8:7).	A time to love and a time to hate (Rom. 12:9–10).
A time to plant and a time to pluck up what was planted (Matt. 10:14).	A time to embrace and a time to refrain from embracing (Rom. 10:11, MSG).	A time for war and a time for peace (Luke 22:52–53).
A time to kill and a time to heal (Matt. 5:11–12).	Scripture reassures us, No one who trust God like this—heart and soul—will ever regret it.	A time for war and a time for peace (Luke 22:52–53).
A time to break down and a time to build up (2 Cor. 10:3–5).	A time to seek and a time to lose (Mark 8:35).	
	A time to keep and a time to throw away (Phil. 3:7).	

27

Watch Night/New Year's Day
To Everything There Is a Season
Ecclesiastes 3:1–15

There is a season and a time for all things under heaven. Most likely we will experience each of these seasons during our lifetime. God has place a rhythmic order within us and within the world. But God determines the time.

Time to be born and a time to die. "Very truly, I tell you, unless a grain of wheat falls into the earth and dies, it remains just a single grain; but if it dies, it bears much fruit" (John 12:24). Our first thought is birth and death; the circle of life. We must learn to die to self and accept God's will for our lives. Only then will we be able to bear fruit.

Time to plant and a time to pluck up what was planted. "If anyone will not welcome you or listen to your words, shake off the dust from your feet as you leave that house or town" (Matt. 10:14). We are to plant the word of God wherever we go, but if the word is not welcomed, we are to leave as if plucking up the word.

Time to kill and a time to heal. "Blessed are you when people revile you and persecute you and utter all kinds of evil against you falsely on my account. Rejoice and be glad, for your reward is great in heaven, for in the same way they persecuted the prophets who were before you" (Matt. 5:11–12). Words can either encourage and comfort us or they can kill our spirit. We must choose our words carefully. Once said, they cannot be retracted.

Time to break down and a time build up. "Indeed, we live as human beings but we do not wage war according to human standards; for the weapons of our warfare are not merely human but they have divine power to destroy strongholds. We destroy arguments and every proud obstacle raised up against the knowledge of God, and we take every thought captive to obey Christ" (2 Cor. 10:3–5). We must break down the walls of insecurity in our minds and replace them with God's word for us and to us.

Time to weep and a time to laugh. "For his anger is but for a moment; his favor is for a lifetime. Weeping may linger for the night, but joy comes with the morning" (Ps. 30:5). There will be seasons of tears, but during those seasons, our hope and our joy is found in the strength of the Lord. We are to put our trust and faith in him.

Time to mourn and a time to die. "You have turned my mourning into dancing; you have taken off my sackcloth and clothed me with joy" (Ps. 30:11). Only Jesus can remove the sackcloth of sadness and in its place give us dancing shoes.

Time to throw away stones and a time to gather them together. "When they kept on questioning him, he straightened up and said to them, 'Let anyone among you who is without sin be the first to throw a stone at her'" (John 8:7). The season will come when we must decide to condemn or have mercy. We should keep in mind a season of stone throwing will come to us. If we show mercy, mercy will be shown to us.

Time to embrace and a time to refrain from embracing. "With your whole being you embrace God setting things right, and then you say it, right out loud: 'God has set everything right between him and me!'" (Rom. 10:11, MSG). We must embrace the precepts of God until they become a part of us, body and soul. No one is ever disappointed if they trust God and embrace him.

Time to seek and a time to lose. "For those who want to save their life will lose it, and those who lose their life for my sake, and for the sake of the gospel [a] will save it" (Mark 8:35). We must lose the "me attitude" and seek the will of God.

Time to keep and a time to throw away. "Yet whatever gains I had, these I have come to regard as loss because of Christ" (Phil. 3:7). We need to throw away all our "stuff" as it has no value. What we retain is our relationship with God the Father, God the Son, and God the Holy Spirit.

Time to tear and a time to sew. "Yet even now, says the Lord, return to me with all your heart, with fasting, with weeping, and with mourning; rend your hearts and not your clothing. Return to the Lord, your God, for he is gracious and merciful, slow to anger, and abounding in steadfast love and relents from punishing" (Joel 2:12–13). In biblical times, tearing your clothes was associated with mourning, grief, and loss. More important than outward shows of grief are true sorrow for sin and genuine repentance of the heart.

Time to keep silence and a time to speak. "I was silent and still; I held my peace to no avail; my distress grew worse, my heart became hot within me. While I mused, the fire burned; then I spoke with my tongue" (Ps. 39:2–3). We must learn when we need to speak up and speak out and when to not say a word.

Time to love and a time to hate. "Let love be genuine; hate what is evil, hold fast to what is good; love one another with mutual affection; outdo one another in showing honor" (Rom. 12:9–10). We are to love with God's love, therefore we hate injustice and evil in the world.

Time for war and a time for peace. "Then Jesus said to the chief priests, the officers of the temple police, and the elders who had come for him, 'Have you come out with swords and clubs as if I were a bandit? When I was with you day after day in the temple, you did not lay hands on me'" (Luke 22:52–53). There are many battles to be fought in this world without going to battle against another person. Let's change our mind-set and think about war on poverty, homelessness, drugs, injustices of all kinds.

Whatever season we may find ourselves in, know just like Esther, maybe we were born for such times as this.

STEPPING
INTO
EPIPHANY

	Epiphany Year B Matthew 2:1–12 Home by Another Way	
Ever read your horoscope? Today we look not at astrology but at some astronomers who wondered about a star.	Everything about their visit foreshadowed the life and mission of Christ.	What does it mean for us to leave the manger of Christmas and go home by a different way?
Ever had a light bulb and aha moment where something once so confusing suddenly made sense?	In ancient days all men believed in astrology; man's future and destiny were settled by the star under which he was born.	It is at Bethlehem we encounter Jesus and have an epiphany. We change, we are transformed, and our life is lived in a different way.
Epiphany—a moment in which you suddenly see or understand something in a clear or new way.	Both wise men and Herod wanted to know where the child is, but for different reasons: wise men to worship, Herod to destroy.	We're new, new perspective, new way of seeing things more clearly.
Today is referred to as Epiphany of the Lord. Also called twelfth night celebrates the visit of the Magi.	First time Gentiles come to Jesus foreshadowed what was to happen when Jewish leaders rejected Christ (Isa. 60:6).	
A Christmas Carol by Dickens visited by ghost of Christmas past, present, and future. Ebenezer has an epiphany	Gifts foreshadowed future. Gold symbol of divinity. Frankincense—priesthood Myrrh—Crucifixion.	
Think of the visit of the Wise Men as a visit from the ghost of Christmas future, what was to be.	After the visit the wise men had an epiphany. Warned to find another way home. Bethlehem is not the end of the journey but beginning.	

Epiphany of the Lord Year B
Home by Another Way
Matthew 2:1–12

In Charles Dickens' *A Christmas Carol*, the ghost of Jacob Marley visits his partner Ebenezer Scrooge on the night of Christmas Eve. Scrooge was later visited by the ghost of Christmas past, then Christmas present, and finally Christmas future. In the end, Scrooge has an epiphany. He suddenly sees and understands his life in a clear and new way. Well, we might think of the visit of the wise men as a visit from the ghosts of Christmas future, what was to be. Everything about their visit foreshadowed the life and mission of Christ.

In those ancient days, all men believed in astrology. They believed the future was told from the stars, and they believed a man's destiny was settled by the star under which he was born. The wise men were astrologers. They studied the stars so they would have been aware of something different about the sky, about that star so they traveled long and far to see where royalty had been born. This was the first time Gentiles would come to Jesus. This foreshadowed what was to happen when the Jewish leaders rejected Christ.

The wise men and Herod wanted to know where to find the child but for different reasons. The wise men wanted to worship the child; Herod wanted to destroy him. The gifts presented to the child foreshadowed his future.

Gold is a symbol of divinity and is mentioned throughout the Bible. The gift of gold to the Christ child was symbolic of his divinity—King of kings and Lord of lords; God in the flesh.

Frankincense is a highly fragrant white resin or gum used in worship. Exodus 30:34 talks of it being placed before the covenant in the tent of meeting where God would meet with Moses. God further instructs that it is made not for the individual but is regarded as holy to the Lord. Frankincense is a symbol of holiness and righteousness. The gift of frankincense to the Christ child was symbolic of his priesthood and being set aside as holy to the God.

Myrrh was a spice and was used in embalming. It was also mingled with wine to form an article of drink. Mark 15:23 tells us that such a drink was given to Christ when he was about to be crucified. Myrrh symbolized bitterness, suffering, and affliction. The gift of myrrh was symbolic of Jesus's Crucifixion.

The wise men were warned in a dream to go home by another route or another way. When we encounter Jesus, we too leave in a different way. We are changed, transformed. Once we encounter Jesus we cannot leave as the same person. If we are aware of the potential, every encounter with Jesus requires us to go a different way; maybe by a different way, but for sure in a different way.

Baptism of the
Lord Year B
Mark 1:–11
Have You Been
to the Jordan?

All the Judean countryside and all of Jerusalem went to John to be baptized for repentance of the forgiveness of sins.

John's message did not focus on him but the one who would come after him.

Jesus was baptized in the Jordan to show an outward response to an inward reordered life. As it runs through Israel, the Jordan runs throughout the Bible.

Repentance—to change the mind concerning former beliefs and behaviors. For Jews it meant turning from Judaism.

It was customary for a servant to remove the sandals of a visitor and wash his feet. John said he was not worthy to even do this menial task for Jesus.

It was in the Jordan where Joshua had the twelve priests to stand so the Israelites could cross over into the promised land.

John was a fashion statement right out of GQ magazine. Was on latest fad diet. He was hip. He had it all together.

Luke's gospel tells us that Jesus prayed and was baptized. The presence of the Trinity at Jesus's baptism.

It was in the Jordan where Elijah and Elisha crossed over on dry ground and where Elisha had Naaman the leper to bathe so he would be cured.

God was pleased with Jesus before he won victory over temptation, started his ministry, called his disciples and apostles.

Jesus is our Jordan.

God was pleased with Jesus before he cured and healed many, performed many miracles, submitted his will for God's will and before he gave his life for all.

35

Baptism of the Lord Year B
Have You Been to the Jordan?
Mark 1:4–11

People from the whole Judean countryside and *all* the people of Jerusalem were going out to John to be baptized. John the Baptizer proclaimed baptism of repentance for the forgiveness of sin. Repentance (Gk. metanoia) literally means "to change the mind." It refers to changing the mind regarding former beliefs and behaviors. This change is what John's baptism meant to the Jewish people. When they came to be baptized by John in the Jordan, they were turning away from Judaism. In this way, repentance and baptism are a way of turning away from the past and turning toward a new life for the future.

John was a fashion statement right out of *GQ* magazine. He was dressed in camel hair, a forerunner to the camel hair sports coat, and wore a leather belt. The only thing missing was a designer tag. He was wearing what all the best dressed prophets were wearing (2 Kings 1:8, Zech. 13:4). He was also on the latest fad diet of locust and wild honey. John was hip. He had his act together.

John the Baptizer's message did not focus on him but the one who would come after him. John described him as being more powerful than he. It was customary for a servant to stoop down, untie the sandal and wash the feet of a visitor to his master's home. John described himself as not being worthy to even perform this menial task for Jesus.

Luke's gospel tells us Jesus prayed and was baptized. When John baptized Jesus in the Jordan, the heavens were torn apart and the Spirit descended like a dove on Jesus. And a voice came from heaven, "You are my Son, the Beloved, with you I am well pleased." Notice the presence of the Trinity: God the Father, God the Son, and God the Spirit. The word *pleased* means think well of, approve. God approved of Jesus and thought well of him before he survived the temptation in the wilderness; before he began his ministry, before he had disciples, before he called the apostles, before he cured many and healed the sick, before he performed miracles, before he submitted his will to God's will, and before he gave his life for all. God also thinks well of us and approves of us before we begin our calling and doing what we were created to do. We are his children. We too are his beloved.

Jesus was baptized in the Jordan to show an outward sign of an inward reordered life. Just as it runs through Israel as an important source for watering a dry land, the Jordan also runs through the Bible with an even greater spiritual status. Many miracles had taken place in the Jordan. One was when Joshua had the twelve priests with the Ark of the Covenant stand in the Jordan making the water stop flowing. All of the Israelites were able to cross over on dry ground into the promised land.[9] It was also at the Jordan that Elijah and Elisha walked through on dry ground[10] and where Elisha had Naaman bathe in the Jordan so he would be healed of leprosy[11].

Jesus is our Jordan. He is our way into the Holy Land and it is through him that we are cleansed and healed of all our brokenness.

---

[9] Joshua 3–6
[10] 2 Kings 2:8
[11] 2 Kings 5

	Epiphany 2 Year B John 1:43–51 Anything Good	
Philip tells Nathanael they had found the Lord's Messiah, the one Moses in the Law and the prophets wrote about.	Starting with verse 19, John the Baptist cries out in the wilderness make straight the way of the Lord.	Philip takes Nathanael to Jesus where Nathanael declares Jesus as rabbi, Son of God and King of Israel.
What had Philip seen that he also wanted Nathanael to see?	In verse 29 John sees Jesus and proclaims he is the Lamb of God who takes away the sin of the world.	A changed had taken place in Nathanael. He no longer questioned if anything good could come out of Nazareth.
What we learn in previous verses in Chapter 1.	In verse 35 John again proclaims Jesus as the Lamb of God, and two of his disciples follow Jesus. In verse 43 Jesus decides to go to Galilee and he finds Philip.	Sometimes we have a "Can anything good" attitude. Can anything good come out of that family, that side of town, or that school?
	Philip has seen many people's lives changed when they encountered Jesus. His own life was changed. He wanted Nathanael to experience the same.	Do we limit people because can anything good come from someone who dresses like that, or has piercing and tattoos or a sordid past?
		Jesus looks at the heart. We should go and do likewise.

Epiphany 2 Year B
Anything Good
John 1:43–51

In our scripture, like Jesus we find Nathanael sitting in under a fig tree. When Philip came to him and announced they had found the one that Moses in the Law and the prophets wrote about. Although we don't know Nathanael's facial expression, we can hear it in his words, "Can anything good come out of Nazareth?" Philip invited him to come and see. What had Philip seen that he also wanted Nathanael to see?

Previously in Chapter 1 starting in verse 19, we find John the Baptist proclaiming who he wasn't and who he was. He pronounced the coming of the Lord's Messiah. The next day, John sees Jesus and openly declares him "The Lamb of God who take away the sin of the world." John testifies to the Spirit descending from heaven like a dove and it remained on Jesus. He further proclaimed Jesus as the Son of God.

The next day we hear John proclaim Jesus as the Lamb of God, and two of John's disciples followed Jesus. One of those disciples was Andrew who went and told his brother Simon they had found the Lord's Messiah, and Simon was changed including his name to Cephas. There were others who had made the decision to believe Jesus was the Lord's Messiah and to follow Jesus. The crowds were growing.

The following day and Jesus decides to go to Galilee where he found Philip and said, "Follow Me." Philip was changed and made the decision to follow Jesus. He went to tell Nathanael. Now Nathanael is sitting under a fig tree.

We sometimes need to check our attitude at the door and be more accepting. Have we ever thought, can anything good come out of "that side of town" or "that school" or "that family"?

Do we limit people because of their outward appearance including piercings and tattoos, the type of house in which they live, or the color of their skin? Jesus accepts all people because he knows their hearts. We should go and do likewise.

Epiphany 3 Year B Mark 1:14–20		
Tell a fishing story		
We find the account of Jesus calling the first disciples in Matthew, Mark, and Luke.	Peter and Andrew were brothers. James and John were brothers.	Why were they the first chosen? Each set of brothers would have lived in the same environment. Each set of brothers would understand one another.
One account builds upon another. Matthew used four verses. Mark used six verses, and Luke used ten verses.	All four of them were from Bethsaida.	All four were from the small fishing town of Bethsaida. They would have had similar childhood experiences.
Two or more witnesses are needed to get the full account.	All four were fishermen and were in business together. Mark reveals it was a lucrative business as James and John had hired hands.	All four were business partners, so they already had a working relationship.
		All four were fisherman, and fisherman had to have patience. The gift of patience would be needed for this new ministry.
		What are we currently doing that we could do for the Lord? God is calling us to join him in ministry. Will we leave our nets and follow?

Epiphany 3 Year B
A Band of Brothers
Mark 1:14–20

I only have two fishing stories to tell. The first one I was in grade school when I went fishing with my sister and one of our cousins. I caught my sister's blouse with my sister still in it. The next and last time I went fishing was in college trying to impress a guy. He had a brand-new rod and reel which he allowed me to use. I caught a tree, and the line was so tangled he had to cut the rod and reel out of the tree. After that I gave up fishing. This may have been some of the luck that Peter, Andrew, James, and John were having, which resulted in them leaving it all behind to follow Jesus.

We find the account of Jesus calling the first four disciples in Matthew, Mark, and Luke. Each one is told with one being more detailed than the other. What Matthew[12] told in four verses, Mark[13] tells in six, and good old Dr. Luke[14] tells in ten verses. Also, Mark tells the story sooner than Matthew or Luke. Do not get "hung up" on these different accounts. The spine or backbone is the same in each account while the ribs are the details. The Law of Moses required at least two witnesses and that was so they could get all of the information. Some of us are detailed people, others like my husband are the *Reader's Digest* version, and others fall in the middle of the road ver-

---

12 Matthew 4:18–22
13 Mark 1:14–20
14 Luke 5:1–11

sion. But through these accounts, we get a pretty good idea of what happened at the calling of these first disciples.

Jesus was by the Sea of Galilee and saw two brothers, fishermen, Peter and Andrew, and invited them to follow him and fish for people instead of fish. They left immediately. Jesus saw two other fishermen who were brothers, James and John, and they left immediately also to follow Jesus and fish for people.

We also learn that these four fishermen are from the same town, Bethsaida and they were partners in the fishing industry. They left their families behind, laid down their nets, docked their boats, left their livelihood behind, and followed Jesus.

Jesus called Peter, Andrew, James, and John to be his first disciples. He called them because they were brothers. Each set of brothers were tied to one another through the same childhood experiences.

Jesus called them because they were partners in business. They already had a working relationship with one another and a common goal: to catch fish. They had a lucrative business as they had hired hands.

Jesus called them because they were from the same town. The four of them would have similar backgrounds and experiences. They had been friends for a long time. They had grown up together.

Jesus also called four fishermen because fishermen were known for their patience. They can sit all day in a boat without catching any fish only to return the next day to the same location and prepare to sit it out again. Jesus knew that the first disciples would need to be patient; love is patient. He knew theses disciples were changing their life goals and they would need to be dedicated to the call, which takes patience and longevity.

Is Jesus calling us to leave our so-called nets and follow him? Of course, he is. There is something he sees in you that is needed for his ministry. There is something you are currently doing that could be used for the Lord. Knowing this and having a relationship with Jesus makes it easy to leave all behind and start a new life following Jesus.

	Epiphany 4 Year B Mark 1:21–28 Strange Things Going On in Church	
What is strange in one church is normal in another.	Unclean spirit knew Jesus and called him Jesus from Nazareth	What is an unclean spirit? One that is not clean.
They—Jesus and the four fisherman disciples—set off to Capernaum.	Unclean spirit questioned Jesus.	We each have them: obsession, abuse, greed, gossip, etc.
On the Sabbath, Jesus taught with authority in the synagogue. Could it be instead of the law taught by the scribes, Jesus taught transformation.	Unclean spirit confessed Jesus as the Holy One of God.	We need to go to Jesus. Ask him questions. Then confess he is the Holy One of God.
In the middle of the service, a man entered with an unclean spirit.		When we do, we will be transformed. Stranger things have happened.

Epiphany 4 Year B
Strange Things Going On in Church
Mark 1:21–28

Have you ever had something strange happen at church, during a worship service? What would be strange in one service is normal in another. As for us Methodists, we don't experience the strange. We have a hard time standing when we sing "Standing on the Promises" or "Stand up for Jesus." But there are probably strange things going on in which we are not aware.

Our scripture lesson starts out with "they," which refers to Jesus and his newly appointed fishermen disciples: Peter, Andrew, James, and John. They traveled to Capernaum, and on the Sabbath, they went to the synagogue and Jesus taught not like the scribes but with authority. We are not told what he taught but could it possibly be instead of the Law he was teaching transformation? The people were sitting up and listening. A man with an unclean spirit appeared and the unclean spirit spoke up, right in the middle of the message. The unclean spirit called Jesus, Jesus of Nazareth. The uncleaned spirit questioned Jesus, asking if he was going to destroy them. The unclean spirit told him he knew he was the Holy One of God. Jesus rebuked the unclean spirit and told him to be silent and to come out and he did.

What is an unclean spirit? A spirit that has not been cleaned. That may sound a little simplistic at first, but let's dig a little deeper. In Old Testament times the ordinary state of most things was "cleanness," but a person or thing could contract ritual "uncleanness" or "impurity" in a variety of ways: by skin diseases, discharges of bodily fluids, touching something dead, or eating unclean foods.[15] An unclean person in general had to avoid that which was holy and take steps to return to a state of cleanness. Uncleanness placed a person in a "dangerous" condition under threat of divine retribution, even death of the person approached the sanctuary.[16] "Unclean" objects required purification by water or fire or were destroyed depending on the material.[17]

Today we think of unclean spirits in a different way. We may have an unclean spirit of addiction. This could range anywhere from chocolate, to drugs to Facebook or Amazon Prime. We may have an unclean spirit of greed where we not only want more but believe we deserve more.

We may have an unclean spirit of gluttony where we supersize our way through life. We may have an unclean spirit of gossip. We can try to describe gossip as a prayer request, but deep down we know the difference. We may have an unclean spirit of a mental or emotional disorder where we continuously wear masks so no one will know. And there are many more we could name.

The man with the unclean spirit went to Jesus. A friend didn't take him, a priest didn't take him, his coworkers didn't take him, his synagogue family didn't take him, but he took himself to Jesus of Nazareth. He confessed that Jesus was the Holy One of God. Jesus rid him of the unclean spirit.

Whatever unclean spirit may have us in chains, we need to take ourselves to Jesus and confess that Jesus is the Holy One of God. This is when and where transformation begins.

---

[15] Numbers 5:2, Leviticus 11, Deuteronomy 14
[16] Leviticus 15:31
[17] Leviticus 11:32–25, Number 31:21–33

	Epiphany 5 Year B Mark 1:29–39 The Power of a Touch	
Previous scripture, Jesus selected first four disciples, taught with authority, healed with authority.	Was more important to her to serve than to keep the Sabbath holy. Hospitality was a huge part of their culture.	Scriptures about serving who (Matt. 23:11–12), what (Col. 3:17).
Simon's mother-in-law sick in bed with fever. Was not able to be a good hostess.	Don't become Pharisees thinking we must strictly obey the law but rather the intent of the law. What could be holier than loving God through serving others?	Where (John 12:26) Why (Mark 10:45)
Jesus healed with only a touch. She got up and began to serve. Serve is same word as Mark uses in the resurrection of Jesus.	Jesus was teaching we do not have to wait until the Sabbath is over to be healed.	How (Gal. 5:13) How can we? (1 Pet. 4:10)
Serve used to describe the angles ministering to Jesus in wilderness. Serve—caring for the needs of others in an active, practical way as the Lord guides.		In the words of Dianna Ross

Epiphany 5 Year B
The Power of a Touch
Mark 1:29–39

Previous to today's scripture reading, Jesus called his first four disciples—Simon, Andrew, James, and John—who went with him to Capernaum. On the Sabbath they all went into the synagogue and Jesus began to preach and taught with authority. Then he healed a man with an unclean spirit with authority. They left the synagogue and immediately went to Simon and Andrew's house.

Simon's mother-in-law was sick in bed with a fever. She was probably embarrassed because she could not serve as the role of hostess. Jesus went to her, took hold of her hand, and lifted her up. That's what Jesus does. He lifts up, not put down.

The Greek word for lifts up is the same word used in Jesus's resurrection in Mark 16:6. No spoken words are recorded. He just took her hand and she got up. Then she began to serve them. The Greek work for serve is the same word that Mark uses to relate what the angels did to Jesus when he was in the wilderness. The transliteration of serve is "caring for the needs of others in an active, practical way, as the Lord guides." Service should be our response to what Jesus does in our life.

To this woman, it was more important to keep the intent of the law by serving on the Sabbath than to adhere to its strict requirements. We do not want to be like the Pharisees and be so intent on keeping the law that we forget what the law is really about. Simon's mother-in-law chose service above the sacredness of the Sabbath. Jesus is teaching here that it is not necessary to wait until the Sabbath is over to be healed. What could be holier than loving God by serving others?

Let's see what scripture says about serving.

- **Who**: "The greatest among you will be your servant. All who exalt themselves will be humbled, and all who humble themselves will be exalted" (Matt. 23:11–12).
- **What**: "And whatever you do, in word or deed, do everything in the name of the Lord Jesus, giving thanks to God the Father through him" (Col. 3:17).
- **Where**: "Whoever serves me must follow me, and where I am, there will my servant be also. Whoever serves me, the Father will honor" (John 12:26).
- **Why**: "For the Son of Man came not to be served but to serve, and to give his life a ransom for many" (Mark 10:45).
- **How**: "For you were called to freedom, brothers and sisters; only do not use your freedom as an opportunity for self-indulgence, but through love become slaves to one another" (Gal. 5:13).
- **How Can We**: "Like good stewards of the manifold grace of God, serve one another with whatever gift each of you has received" (1 Pet. 4:10).

Dianna Ross summed it up like this:

> Take a little time out of your busy day
> To give encouragement
> To someone who's lost the way
> Or would I be talking to a stone
> If I asked you
> To share a problem that's not your own
> We can change things if we start giving
> If you see an old friend on the street
> And he's down
> Remember his shoes could fit your feet
> Try a little kindness you'll see

LILLITH O'SHANN EDMISTON MOORE

It's something that comes very naturally
We can change things if we start giving
Reach out and touch
Somebody's hand
Make this world a better place
If you can.
And we all can.

	Transfiguration Year B Mark 9:2–9 Where the Law and the Prophets Intersect the Gospel	
Previously, Jesus asked who people said he was. Disciples answered John the Baptist, Elijah, a prophet.	Jesus takes Peter, James, and John up to a high mountain by themselves.	What does the transfiguration mean to us? Life after death in a different form.
Jesus asked the disciples who they said he was. Peter answered the Christ.	Jesus was transfigured. Metamorphoo—change form keeping inner reality. Think of a caterpillar transforming into a butterfly.	Answer the question of who Jesus was, is, and will be.
	Moses and Elijah appear and talk with Jesus. Wouldn't you have loved to hear what they said?	The cross of the gospel is composed of the Law and the prophets which intersect to form the gospel.
	Then "the Voice" saying, This is my Son, the beloved. Listen to him.	Where do they intersect? At the heart of the sacrificial cross of Christ Jesus.

Transfiguration Year B
Where the Law and Prophets Intersects the Gospel
Mark 9:2–9

Previously in chapter 8, verses 27–30, Jesus and his disciples were going to villages of Caesarea Philippi and along the way Jesus questioned them, "Who do people say I am?" They replied, "Some say John the Baptist, some say Elijah and others say one of the prophets."

Then Jesus asked, "Who do you say I am?" Peter responded, "You are the Christ!" So, Jesus knew he was the talk of the town and there was indecision as to his identity.

In our scripture lesson for today, six days have passed, and Jesus brought Peter, James, and John to a high mountain by themselves and was transfigured before them. The Greek word for transfigured is *metamorphoo* (sound familiar), which means changing form while keeping with inner reality. Think of a caterpillar changing into a butterfly. *Metamorphoo* is the root word for metamorphosis. We are transformed into the same image excellence that shines in Christ.

> And all of us, with unveiled faces, seeing the glory of the Lord as though reflected in a mirror, are being transformed into the same image from one degree of glory to another; for this comes from the Lord, the Spirit. (2 Cor. 3:18)

When Jesus was transfigured, his garments became dazzling white as no one on earth could bleach them even using Clorox. Then suddenly, Moses and Elijah appear and are talking to Jesus. (Wouldn't you have loved to have heard that conversation?) So there is life after death, but we are transfigured to another form. They must have been in some form that allowed Peter, James, and John to recognize them. Of course, Peter just had to be the one to speak up, offering to build three dwellings or tabernacles. Then a cloud overshadowed them, and they heard the voice (you know the one) say, "This is my Son, the beloved. Listen to him." Then Jesus was alone.

What does the transfiguration mean to us? On one side we have Moses who represents the Law and the other side we have Elijah who represents the prophets, and in the middle, we have Jesus who is the Gospel, the Word, the one who did not come to abolish the Law but to fulfill it and to fulfill prophecy. We have the voice of God affirming that Jesus is the Christ, his beloved Son, and wanting us to listen to him. There had been questions about the identity of Jesus. The transfiguration took place to show who he was not and who he was. He was Messiah, God's Son transfigured into human form so he could walk this earth and show us the way.

Where does the Law and the prophets intersect? At the sacrificial cross of Jesus Christ, right at his heart. Jesus is the heart of the gospel. We should take the gospel to heart so that we too can be transformed and transfigured into a light to shine in this dark and perverse world.

STEPPING
INTO
LENT

	Ash Wednesday Year B Matthew 6:1–6, 16–21 Christian Discipleship	
Continue with Sermon on the Mount. Jesus is teaching a crowd of his disciples about Christian discipleship.	Next principle of discipleship is praying. We have gotten God confused with Santa Claus. Don't give God a to-do list.	We should fast from ourselves and take care of the less fortunate.
Beware of practicing your piety. Piety is someone's inner response to the things of God which naturally expresses itself in reverence for God.	Prayer is the discipline the disciples asked Jesus to teach them.	Next principle of discipleship is store up heavenly rewards not earthly ones. Christian discipleship should be done in secret.
Proper piety is characterized by godly behavior and the end result is that God is glorified.	Pray the prayer that never fails: "Thy will be done on earth as in heaven."	The Father will see in secret and will reward us in heaven. This is what it means to store up treasures in heaven. That is where our hearts are.
Do not do acts of piety to impress others. You may receive earthly applause and praise, but God will not be clapping.	Next principle of discipleship is fasting. Don't make a big show of your sacrifices to God.	Our challenge—where is our heart? Would we continue to serve God if no one appreciated us for it, if we received criticism for our obedience?
Principles of discipleship. Jesus teaches us *when* we give, *when* we pray, *when* we fast. It's not an option, it's a *command*.	"Is not this the fast that I choose; loose the bonds of injustice, undo thongs of the yoke, let oppressed go free, break every yoke. Is it not to share your bread with the hungry, bring the homeless, poor into your house, when you see the naked, cover them and not hide yourself from your own kin?" (Isa. 58:6–7).	What if no one did anything in return for us, would we still do acts of kindness, worship, and justice?
		If we wouldn't receive approval from the one person whose approval we crave, would we still serve others? Show love for God and others.

Ash Wednesday Year B
Christian Discipleship
Matthew 6:1–6, 16–21

Our scripture reading for today continues with Jesus's Sermon on the Mount which started in Chapter 4, verse 23. According to Luke 6:17, it wasn't just the twelve apostles but a great crowd of his disciples and a multitude of people from all Judea, Jerusalem, and the coast of Tyre and Sidon. Jesus is teaching the principals of Christian discipleship.

First, we must beware of practicing our piety. Piety is someone's inner response to the things of God which naturally expresses itself in reverence for God. Proper piety is characterized by godly behavior and the end result is God glorified. So do not do acts of piety just to show off to others what you have done. You may receive earthly applause and praise, but you will not hear God clapping. He is more interested in the why you are doing instead of what or how much.

The next principle of Christian discipleship that Jesus teaches is *when* you give, *when* you pray, *when* you fast. It doesn't say *if* you give, pray, or fast. There is no option. This is a not a request. This is Christian living.

The next principle of Christian discipleship is stewardship. Alms are gifts prompted by love given to those in need. We must give of who we are and what we have, not what we have left over. We learn to live below our means, live less comfortably so that the poor may live. Faith and finances go hand in hand. What you do with your checkbook is just as important as what you do with your Bible. God blesses us so that we may bless others.

The next principle of Christian discipleship is praying. Prayer is communion with God, not a performance. Most of us do not know how to pray. Somehow, we have gotten God confused with Santa Claus. We give Santa our wish list and we give God are to-do list. We tell him all that is going on and then proceed to tell him what he needs to do about it and then we wait for it to happen. No wonder so many people are disappointed in praying and become disillusioned about prayer. Prayer is the only discipline the disciples asked Jesus to teach them. And what did he teach them? The prayer that never fails: "thy will be done on earth as it is in heaven." Prayer is praising and worshipping God. It is finding peace in the midst of troubles, calm in a storm, love in the midst of loneliness, direction at a crossroad. It is trusting God completely so that we can sincerely say, "thy will be done on earth as it is in heaven."

The next principle of Christian discipleship Jesus taught his disciples was fasting. Don't make a big show of it or call attention to self when we make sacrifices in Jesus's name.

> Is not this the fast that I choose: to loose the bonds of injustice, to undo the thongs of the yoke, to let the oppressed go free, and to break every yoke? Is it not to share your bread with the hungry, and bring the homeless poor into your house; when you see the naked, to cover them, and not to hide yourself from your own kin? (Isa. 58:6–7)

All of these are acts of piety. We should fast from ourselves and take care of those less fortunate.

The next principle of Christian discipleship is to store up heavenly rewards, not earthly ones. Christian discipleship should be done in secret. Don't put on a big production about what we are doing in the name of Jesus Christ. Just do it without telling anyone. The Father sees in secret and he will reward us in heaven. This is what it means to store up treasures in heaven where moth or rust can't consume them. Don't set your eyes on earthly rewards but for those that are eternal.

Our challenge for today is, where is our heart? Would we continue to serve God if no one appreciated us for it? What if all we received was criticism for our obedience to God? Or what if no one did something for us in return? Would we still do acts of kindness, acts of worship, and acts of justice? If we couldn't impress that one person whom we crave their approval, would we still obey? Practice Christian discipleship by showing your love for God and others which fulfills the greatest commandment of all.

	Lent 1 Year B Mark 1:9–15 God Allows Turns	
Mark gives us the Reader's Digest version of Jesus's baptism, temptation, and beginning of the Galilean ministry.	Jesus taken immediately out into the wilderness, not just the outskirts. Didn't have time to decide what to take and what to leave. He was there forty days.	Jesus ministry began after John was arrested. Jesus preached good news of God, which is the coming kingdom of God.
Jesus's first public appearance was at his baptism. Others were being baptized (Luke 3:21).	From other Gospels we learn Satan tempted Jesus by quoting scripture and Jesus fought back with scripture.	Wesley states kingdom of God is a condition of the soul, a matter of the heart.
He needed to display a public repentance so others would see and take his message and ministry seriously.	Jesus took nothing, but God provided all he needed: his word.	Jesus preached repentance, and belief in the good news of God.
Trinity present at Jesus's baptism. Heavens tore apart, Spirit descended and voice said, You are my Son, the Beloved, with you I am well pleased.	In this life we will have many trips to the wilderness. Most times we carry our baggage with us. It is in the wilderness that we leave our baggage.	Repent—stop going in one direction, turn completely around and go in another direction.
	When we experience life without luggage, we discover we are free from it; no longer has power over us.	Lent is a time to spend in the wilderness, face our demons, and leave our baggage behind. God does allow U-turns.

Lent 1 Year B
God Allows U-Turns
Mark 1:9–15

Our scripture reading for today is Mark's Reader's Digest version of Jesus's baptism, his temptation, and the beginning of his Galilean ministry.

Jesus made his first public appearance when John baptized him in the Jordan River. In Luke's gospel, we learn other people were being baptized for the repentance of sins.[18] Jesus's baptism united him with those John had previously baptized. Jesus was baptized to show he was dedicating his life to righteous living. He needed to display a public repentance so others would see and would take his message and ministry seriously.

When Jesus was baptized, the Trinity was present. When Jesus came up out of the water, he saw the heavens torn apart. The only other time Mark used the word for "torn apart" is in the tearing of the temple curtain when Jesus died.[19] The Spirit descended on him like a dove and he heard God's voice say, "This is my son the Beloved in whom I am well pleased." God's voice confirmed Jesus as his son and was pleased with Jesus because he was his son, not because of anything Jesus had done. We need to know and take it to heart that God is pleased with us because we are his children and we do not have to do anything to win his favor. We are his beloved.

Next the Spirit immediately drove Jesus out into the wilderness. Notice it says out into the wilderness. He didn't drive him to

---

[18] Luke 3:21
[19] Mark 15:38

the beginning of the wilderness, put out, implying way out into the wilderness. And there he stayed for forty days. His only companions were Satan, wild animals, and ministering angels.

Jesus did not use his relationship with God to get out of going into the wilderness. Mark tells us Jesus was immediately in the wilderness. Jesus didn't have time to pack a suitcase or decide what to take or what to leave. From other gospels we learn Satan tempted Jesus by quoting scripture and Jesus fought back using scripture. Jesus took nothing with him yet God provided all he needed, God's word.

In this earthly world, we will have many journeys to the wilderness. Most times we are there before we know it. The sad part is we normally travel with our baggage. It is in the wilderness that we give it up and in the wilderness our baggage is discarded. In order to battle the temptation of clinging to our baggage, we must cling to the Word of God. We must know scripture and what it says and means. This gives us the strength needed for forty days of fasting from our baggage. When we experience life without our luggage for forty days, we discover it no longer has power over us and we really no longer need it as a crutch.

Mark tells us that Jesus's ministry began after John the Baptist was arrested. Jesus came preaching the good news of God, which is the coming kingdom of God. According to John Wesley, the kingdom of God is a condition of the soul, a matter of the heart. Jesus states that the time is fulfilled, and the kingdom of God has come near. Repent and believe in the good news.

Repentance means to stop going in one direction, turn around completely and go the opposite way. It's us agreeing with God that we have sinned, and we take specific action to do God's will. Repentance is not just a wishful desire for change. It is a change of heart and mind as a direct response to God's word.

This time of Lent is a time for us to spend time in the wilderness, face our demons head on, and leave all our baggage at the foot of the cross. It is a time of giving up our old ways and start living the good news of the kingdom of God. It is a time where God allows us to make a U-turn and start over. We must be prepared for the wilderness but also be prepared for our God-chosen ministry.

Lent 2 Year B
Mark 8:31–38
Cost and Demand
of Discipleship

Peter just declared Jesus as Messiah. Now Jesus will teach them just what that means.	Before taking a trip, we check the cost. The same is true with discipleship. We must sit down and figure the cost of being a genuine follower of Christ.	Cost 1. We will suffer. Doing God's will is not always easy.
The Jews expected Messiah to redeem Israel by overthrowing Roman rule. They were expecting an earthly kingdom.	As in economics there is supply and demand; in discipleship there are costs and demands.	Cost 2. We will be rejected. We change and become different persons. Friends may have a problem with the new you.
This is first time Jesus talks about his passion, his suffering. He also spoke of rejection of the religious leaders.	Demand 1. We must set our mind not on human things but divine things (2 Cor. 4:18).	Cost 3. We will lose our lives for Jesus's sake and for the sake of the gospel in order to save our lives. We give up our old life for a new eternal life.
Jesus tells them he will be killed but after three days he would rise again.	Demand 2. We must deny self. Set new priorities. Think and act differently.	Payoff—freedom. Total surrender to Christ results in us becoming a FROG: fully relying on God. Freedom from worry, doubt, sorrow, and pain.
Peter rebukes Jesus for saying these things, and Jesus rebukes Peter while looking at the other disciples.	Demand 3. We must take up our cross. Our cross that we lift and carry is all the injustices of the world.	Are we disciples of Christ? It's time for lip service Christ followers to sit down and count the cost. Are you all in or all out? There are only two choices.
	Demand 4. We must follow Jesus. We must stay close to Jesus and develop his ways and his thoughts.	

Lent 2 Year B
Cost and Demand of Discipleship
Mark 8:31–38

Peter has just declared Jesus as Messiah. Jesus tried to teach them of his impending death.

In the Hebrew language, Messiah means "anointed one" or "chosen one." The Greek equivalent is the word we know as Christ. The name "Jesus Christ" is the same as "Jesus the Messiah." In biblical times, anointing someone with oil was a sign that God was consecrating or setting apart that person for a particular role, a special God-ordained purpose.

The Jews of Jesus's day expected the Messiah to redeem Israel by overthrowing the rule of the Romans and establishing an earthly kingdom.[20] It wasn't until after Jesus's resurrection that his disciples finally began to understand the prophecies in the Old Testament about the Messiah.[21]

In today's reading, this is the first teaching by Jesus to the disciples that the Son of Man must suffer, be rejected by the elders, the chief priests and scribes. He will be killed but after three days he would rise again. Now Peter did not approve of what Jesus said, so Peter rebuked him or criticized him. And of course, Jesus sets Peter straight but looks at the disciples and said, "Get behind me Satan! For you are setting your mind not on divine things but on human things." Then Jesus tells us what we must do if we decide to be a fol-

---

[20] Acts 1:6
[21] Luke 24: 25–27

lower or disciple of his. If you have taken an economics class, you are familiar with the concept of supply and demand. With discipleship there are demands and costs.

Before going on a trip, what is the first thing we do? We run the numbers to see how much it will cost and then decide if we want to sacrifice that amount of money for what we will get out of it. In other words, will it be worth the cost? This is what we must do before we decide to be a disciple, a follower of Christ.

Demand #1. We must set our mind not on human things but on divine things.[22] We must see as God sees. We must focus on eternal things, not the earthly. "So, we fix our eyes not on what is seen, but on what is unseen, since what is seen is temporary, but what is unseen is eternal."[23]

Demand #2. We must deny self.[24] We can no longer think, "What's in it for me?" We must cast ourselves aside and only think of the needs of others. Our focus can no longer be our convenience. We must be willing to sacrifice our interest for what is best for others or the one in need. We must set new priorities.

Demand #3. We must take up our cross.[25] The words "take up" mean to raise up or lift up, to take upon oneself and carry what has been raised, to bear. Our cross is servanthood. We are to take up the cause for justice and see to the needs of the poor, hungry, sick, thirsty, and those in prison.

Demand #4. We must follow Jesus.[26] Do we really know what it means to follow Jesus? It means we stick closely to Jesus, study his word, obey his word, follow his example of the sacrificial life. If he says go left then we go left. If he says jump, we jump. We do what Jesus does. You remember the game follow the leader? When the leader is Jesus, the followers are disciples.

---

[22] Mark 8:33
[23] 2 Corinthians 4:18
[24] Mark 8:34
[25] Ibid.
[26] Ibid.

Cost #1. We will suffer.[27] If we have never suffered for Christ, we're probably not committed disciples. Anyone who has done the will of God knows it is not always easy. When Jesus asks us to step out of the boat, will we? Do we?

Cost #2. We will be rejected.[28] When we follow Jesus, we become a serious disciple of his teachings and his ways; we will have to change a lot of our habits and attitudes. We change, and sometimes that is not received well by those who have known us the longest. Friends may reject us, others may reject the gospel.

Cost #3. We will lose our lives for Jesus's sake and the sake of the gospel in order to save our lives.[29] In order to save our lives as a disciple, we must lose our lives to receive eternal lives. We give up the old life for a new life, a better life.

The Payoff. Total surrender to discipleship results in an indescribable freedom. You become a FROG: fully relying on God. Disciples listen for his direction before they take the first step. Disciples are free from worry because they know God has a plan for their future and he will work all things out for good.[30] Disciples are free from self and become servant of all. There is power in the towel of servanthood.

The question we must ask is, are we disciples of Christ? Have we set our minds on things eternal? Are we denying self? Have we picked up the cross to carry it? Are we close followers of Christ experiencing changes in us and our thoughts and actions? If not, today is the day to sit down and count the cost and demands. Today is the day for lip service Christ followers to make the decision to be all in or all out? There are only two choices.

---

[27] Mark 8:31
[28] Ibid.
[29] Mark 8:35
[30] Jeremiah 29:11, Romans 8:28

	Lent 3 Year B 1 Corinthians 1:18–25 Jesus Is Nuts	
New Restaurant in town. Everyone wants to go check it out.	Jesus was not afraid to show his weirdness	Are you prepared to be *nutty* for the Lord?
New religion in Corinth Abundant Life Eternal Life Lots of Promises	He talked to foreigners Talked to women Healed on Sunday	Paul asked where to find the truly wise, educated, intelligent?
The catch—had to believe in the Cross. Old rugged cross emblem of suffering and shame	He put a new twist on the law. He forgave sins. God was his Father, etc.	Look around We are the called. We are the nobodies. God wants to use us.
God uses the foolish to shame the wise. Some need miracles. Some philosophical wisdom.	Jesus was N U T S—never underestimated the Spirit	Our challenge today is go be weird for the Lord.
To those called—Jesus is ultimate miracle and wisdom. Foolish can only boast in Jesus because they know they can't do it on their own.		

Lent 3 Year B
Jesus Was NUTS
1 Corinthians 1:18–25

Have you ever noticed people's reactions to the news of a new restaurant "coming soon"? I'm from a small rural town and it would be the topic of conversation at every gathering. We would watch in anticipation as the heavy equipment was unloaded at the site of the new restaurant. We keep watch over its progress until the day comes for the grand opening. Then we rush to be one of the firsts to sample the new menu. For several weeks it is impossible to find a parking space or a table. But soon the newness wears off and we are ready for the next big thing.

This is similar to what was happening in Corinth. There was a new religion in town and excitement filled the air. They heard about new life, abundant life, and eternal life and so many other wonderful promises. But there was one catch, a cross.

During this time to be hung on a cross, to be crucified was something shameful. It sure wasn't anything to boast about. As the old hymn states, it was an emblem of suffering and shame. It would be foolish to have a belief based on a cross.

But God uses the foolish things and people to shame the wise. The Corinth Jews looked for signs and miracles. The Greeks relied on philosophical wisdom. They could not make sense of the why of the cross. It seemed foolish to them that a man purposely put himself in a position to be hung on a cross. That wasn't logical. They couldn't connect the dots. The foolish know this as grace.

To those who were called and are still being called, Jesus is the ultimate sign and miracle and wisdom. The foolish are being called because they don't have to reason things out. They just believe in God and they believe God. The foolish can only boast in Jesus because they know they can't do it without him.

Jesus was not afraid to show his weirdness. He talked to foreigners, talked to women, included women in his ministry, he forgave sins and healed on the Sabbath. He even put a new twist on the law.

> You have heard that it was said to those of ancient times, "You shall not murder"; and whoever murders shall be liable to judgment. But I say to you that if you are angry with a brother or sister, you will be liable to judgment.[31]
>
> You have heard that it was said, "You shall not commit adultery." But I say to you that everyone who looks at a woman with lust has already committed adultery with her in his heart.[32]
>
> You have heard that it was said, "You shall love your neighbor and hate your enemy." But I say to you, Love your enemies and pray for those who persecute you.[33]

Jesus was NUTS: He Never Underestimated The Spirit. We would have to be pretty nutty to "love that old cross." But God calls us, the nobodies, the foolish, to spread the message of Jesus and him crucified. We cherish the "Old Rugged Cross" and the empty tomb. For to us, the foolish, it means new life, abundant life, and eternal life. Meanwhile, we wait and talk about "The Grand Opening."

---

[31] Matthew 5:21–22a
[32] Matthew 5:27–28
[33] Matthew 5:43–45a

Lent 4 Year B
John 3:14–21
The House of
Mercy and Grace

Story of the Roller Skates	Anyone who trusts in him is acquitted. He took our judgment andand nailed it to the cross. We just have to believe it and trust it.	You too can turn around and go home. God will receive you with open arms, open mind, and an open heart.
God loves all of us, not just some. His only son took the judgment and punishment for us so that we would have a full life now and an eternal life.	Wheelbarrow Story; Trust vs. Believe. Do you believe I can roll the wheelbarrow on a rope across Niagara Falls? If so, do you trust that I can do it? Then get in.	Remember he does not condemn, he loves. Perfect love cast out fear.
God sent his son to save the world, not to condemn it. There is no condemnation for those in Christ Jesus (Rom. 8:1). God doesn't point out our sins, he forgives them.	It's one thing to believe and another to trust. I trusted my mother. I knew I could turn around and go back home.	Love, mercy, and grace intersected on the cross. We just have to believe and trust it. Run to God's house of mercy, grace, and love. He is waiting.
God is love and just. He wouldn't sacrifice his only son for us and then still accuse us.	Actions of Noah's time required a flood, but mercy provided a Noah who would build an ark as God directed.	
	Justice required a wilderness for Israelites but mercy provided for all their needs. Our actions require justice. Mercy provided Jesus Christ.	

Lent 4 Year B
The House of Mercy and Grace
John 3:14–21

When I was in the fourth grade, I learned a valuable lesson from my mother which later I would understand as justice, mercy, and grace.

I received a pair of roller skates for Christmas. I was so excited, but since we had hardwood floors, my mother told me to never roller skate inside the house. We lived in a tiny rural township. There was a shortage of smooth surfaces. Our blacktopped road would be my only option and I had been told *not* to play in the road. So, I guess in my small mind I reasoned Momma must not realize there was no adequate place outside for me to skate. So I skated in the house. Yes, on the hardwood floors.

Well, my actions required judgment, so I threatened to run away from home. My mother said she would help me pack. With coat on, carrying my suitcase and my roller skates, I left my home to find some place where roller skating was allowed. But at the top of our road was the highway and I had been warned about walking on the highway by myself. I thought about it, but soon realized I had no choice but to return home.

God loves all of us, not just some of us. His only son took the judgment and punishment for us so that we would have a full life now and an eternal life. God sent his only begotten Son not to judge the world but to save it. Romans 8:1 says there is no condemnation for those in Christ Jesus. God doesn't point out our sins, he forgives them.

God loved the world so much he sacrificed his Son for our sins, our wrongdoings. Would he then point a finger at us after this huge sacrifice? No, he wouldn't. Because if that was the case, why did he send his son to die for nothing?

Anyone who trusts in him is acquitted. He took our judgment and nailed it to the cross. We just have to believe it and trust it.

There is a story of a man with a wheelbarrow and rope claiming to be able to roll the wheelbarrow on a rope stretched over Niagara Falls. He asked a spectator if he believed he could do it. The man replied yes. Then the man asked him if he trusted he could do it. Again, the spectator said yes. So the man said to him, okay get in the wheelbarrow. It's one thing to believe and another to trust. We must do both.

I trusted my mother. I knew I could turn around and go back home. When I did, Mother took my suitcase, unpacked it, and placed the suitcase in the closet without one word spoken between us. It was difficult for me to go back home. I knew I had done wrong. Mother knew I had done wrong. My disobedience required punishment. But I trusted my mother to be just. The mercy and grace was a surprise. That was a very valuable lesson I learned that day. Mother showed grace and mercy, and I felt loved.

The actions of the people of Noah's time required a flood, but mercy provided a Noah who would built an ark as God directed. Because he was obedient, Noah and his family were saved, as was the animal kingdom. Justice required a wilderness for Israelites, but mercy provided a pillar of cloud and a pillar of fire for guidance, food, water, and clothes that did not wear out for years. Our actions require justice. There is no need for grace and mercy if there is no justice. Mercy provided Jesus Christ.

You can turn around and go home. God will receive you with open arms, open mind, and an open heart. Remember, he does not condemn, he loves. Perfect love casts our fear.[34]

Jesus took on all our sins and was sacrificed on the cross. Love, grace, and mercy intersect at the cross, right at the heart of Christ Jesus. We just have to believe and trust it. Run to God's house of mercy and grace. He is waiting and watching for you to come home.

---

[34] 1 John 4:18

Lent 5 Year B
John 12:20–33
The Hour

The word about Jesus had gone viral. Talk of the miracles he had performed was spread outside the Jewish community. Now he had raised Lazarus from the dead.	Jesus continued, "Whoever serves me must follow me, and where I am there will my servant be also."	As followers of Christ, we will have many hours that will come, each one more challenging than the last. Will we accept the challenge or deny it?
Some Greeks came to the festival to see Jesus, to meet him. They were Gentiles who had become followers of Jesus. They came to worship.	Jesus came to serve, not to be served. If we are servants bound to Christ, we must go where he goes, even to the cross.	We must be prepared for whatever hour we face. We must stand firmly, knowing God has provided everything we need to overcome.
This mirrors the wise men coming from the East to find Jesus. The promise of international salvation had just been fulfilled.	Ours is a figurative cross. We must die to self; give up our will for God's will. Only then can we bear fruit.	As followers of Christ, we have to come to see Jesus by serving the poor, thirsty, hungry, needy, naked, homeless, and those in prison.
When Jesus was informed by Philip and Andrew of the Greeks wishing to see him, Jesus responded, "The hour has come for the Son of Man to be glorified."	Jesus states he cannot ask to be saved from the hour since it is God's will. Jesus knew the Father had a plan in place, and his only obligation was to play his part.	We see Jesus when we look into the hungry face of a child, shame of the naked, innocence of those in prison of any kind, or desperation of the homeless.
Of course Jesus was speaking about his impending death. He explained his death as a wheat of grain. The grain of wheat must die in order to produce fruit.	Do we know the gifts with which God has blessed us to enable us to play our role in his plan? Are we using these gifts to be in service to the Lord?	If we are to be followers of Christ, we need to go and do likewise to be the least of those who are members of Jesus's family just as if we were doing for him.
	As followers of Christ, we must set aside ourselves in order to serve others. We must die to self, our way, so that we will be obedient to Christ and bear fruit.	

Lent 5 Year B
The Hour
John 12:20–33

The word about Jesus had gone viral. Talk of the miracles he had performed was spreading outside the Jewish communities. Now he had raised Lazarus from the dead. Some Greeks came to the festival to see Jesus, to meet him. They were Gentiles who had become followers of Christ. They had come to worship. This mirrors the wise men from the East following the star in search of the Christ child. The promised international salvation had just been fulfilled.[35]

When Jesus was informed by Philip and Andrew of the Greeks wishing to see him, Jesus responses, "The hour has come for the Son of Man to be glorified." Of course Jesus was speaking of his impending death. He explained his death as a wheat of grain. The grain of wheat must die in order to produce fruit. Jesus continues, "Whoever serves me must follow me and where I am there will my servant be also." Jesus came to serve, not to be served. If we are servants bound to Christ, we must go where he goes, even to the cross. The big difference is ours is a figurative cross. We must die to self, give up our will for God's will. Only then can we bear fruit.

Jesus stated he could not ask to be saved from the hour since it was God's will. Jesus knew the Father had a plan in place and his only obligation was to play his part. Do we know the gifts with which God has blessed us to enable us to play our role in his plan? Are we using these gifts to be in service to the Lord?

---

[35] New Interpreter's Bible p. 1933

As followers of Christ, we must set aside ourselves in order to serve others. We must die to self, our way, so that we will be obedient to Christ and bear fruit. As followers of Christ, we will have many hours that will come, each one more challenging than the last. We will accept the challenge or deny it? Or as my dad used to ask me, "Are you going to fish or cut bait?"

We must be prepared for whatever hour we are currently facing. We must stand firmly, knowing God has provided everything we need to overcome. As followers of Christ, we have to come to see Jesus by serving the poor, thirsty, hungry, needy, naked, homeless, and those in prison of any kind.

We are true servants when we are able to see Jesus when we look into the hungry face of a child, see the shame of the naked, see innocence of those in prison, and the desperation of the homeless. If we are to be followers of Christ, we need to go and do likewise to the least of those who are members of Jesus's family, just as if we were doing for him.[36]

---

[36] Matthew 25:40

	Palm Sunday Year B Philippians 2:5–11 Enough Is Enough	
Death of Billy Graham Each member of the family formed a receiving line and greeted each person that came through the line. He had a wooden casket. Humble.	How can we be of the same mind as Christ? Prayer, study, obedience, and service.	We must empty ourselves and leave behind unnecessary things.
The mind of Christ is having the same love, being in full accord and of one mind.	Through prayer we learn to give God permission to do his will instead of our laundry list of concerns.	Hear the good news. There is enough encouragement in Christ. There is enough consolation from love.
The mind of Christ is doing nothing from selfish ambition but humbly regarding others as better than ourselves.	Through scripture, we learn the character and nature of Christ so we will do the same.	There is enough sharing in the spirit beyond our momentary struggles, beyond the threat of the times in which we live.
The mind of Christ is not looking to our own interest but the interests of others.	Through obedience we learn God provides us with all we need to do his will.	Mind of Christ is a gift from the spirit through justification. Life of love for God and neighbor is the gift of the spirit through sanctification.
The mind of Christ is emptying ourselves, becoming servants and being obedient.	We must empty ourselves of an envious mind for a unified mind. Empty ourselves of a self-centered mind for a servant's mind.	Justification is what God has done for us. Sanctification is what God does in us.
	We must empty ourselves of a stubborn mind for a submissive mind. A confident mind for a humble mind.	God's grace is sufficient. It's always enough.

Palm Sunday Year B
Enough Is Enough
Philippians 2:5–11

The world was saddened upon hearing the news of Reverend Billy Graham's passing. He lived a humble life and he remained humble in death. Each family member formed a receiving line so that each person who came to the visitation would be welcomed. Reverend Graham had requested to be buried in a wooden casket. Humility, just one of the examples of Billy Graham having the mind of Christ.

What does it mean to have the mind of Christ? It is to have the same love as Christ where we strive to be of one accord and of one mind. We no longer are self-centered but other-centered. It is being selfless and humbly think more of others than we do ourselves. We look not to our own interest, what would be best for us, but consider the interests of others and what would be best for most.[37] The mind of Christ is emptying ourselves, becoming servants and being obedient. Having the mind of Christ is having community awareness.

How can we be of the same mind as Christ? It begins with prayers, scripture, obedience, and service. Through prayer we learn to give God permission to do his will instead of our laundry list of concerns. We learn to really mean it when we say, "Thy kingdom come, thy will be done." We no longer are praying from habit.

Through reading, studying, and applying what we learn through scripture, we learn the character and nature of Christ. We begin to

---

[37] Philippians 2:2b

develop the same characteristics as we are transformed. Through this process we look more like Jesus and less like ourselves.

To have the mind of Christ, we must empty ourselves of an envious mind for a unified mind. We must empty ourselves of a self-centered mind for a servant's mind. We must empty ourselves of a stubborn mind for a submissive mind; a confident mind for a humble mind.

Hear the good news. There is enough encouragement in Christ. There is enough consolation from love. There is enough sharing in the spirit beyond the threat of the times in which we live.[38]

The mind of Christ is a gift from the spirit through justification. Love of life for God and neighbor is the gift of the spirit through sanctification. Justification is what God has done for us. Sanctification is what God does in us.[39]

God's grace is sufficient.[40] It's always enough.

---

[38] Philippians 2:3
[39] Wesley Study Bible p. 1441
[40] 2 Corinthians 12:9a

	Good Friday Year B Hebrews 10:16–25 A New and Living Way	
It's A Wonderful Life. Potter is Old Covenant. Bailey is New. Daily sacrifices by priest but "it was impossible for the blood of bulls and goats to take away sins."	Through the blood of Christ, we have confidence to enter the sanctuary by the new and living way.	Because of this new life, we can approach God with a true heart full of the assurance of our faith.
Only the high priest was allowed in the Holy of holies and that was once a year on the Day of Atonement.	Curtain in temple separated God's earthly presence in the Holy of holies from the people. It symbolized sin. Was torn from top to bottom when Jesus said.	Because of this new life we keep a grip on our confession on our unwavering hope found only in and through Christ Jesus.
New Covenant of the Lord; put laws in their hearts and write them on their minds and he would not remember their sins and lawless deeds.	Through Christ's atonement, we are at-one-ment, no longer forbidden to be in God's presence.	Because of this new life we must encourage one another to love, serve, and worship.
Where there is forgiveness of sin, there is no longer any offering for sin.	Where there is forgiveness of sins and lawless deeds, there is no longer any offering for sin. Christ suffered for sins once, for all.	Because of Christ Jesus, it really is a wonderful life. Atta boy, Clarence.
	We can walk right up to God, full of confidence, knowing we are presentable. We have a new living way. We have a new life in Christ Jesus, one of faith, hope, and love.	

Good Friday Year B
New and Living Way
Hebrews 10:16–25

Most of us have watched the movie *It's a Wonderful Life*, staring Jimmy Stewart and Donna Reed. Mr. Potter is the rich suppressing authority in Bedford Falls. All around good guy George Bailey wants a better life for the people of his town. You might say Mr. Potter is the Old Covenant and George Bailey is the New Covenant.

The old covenant was the Ten Commandments written on tablets of stone. It was a bilateral covenant and obedience was expected. If the Hebrews were obedient then God would bless them. The appointed priest would stand day after day making sacrifices for the community. But it was impossible for the blood of bulls and goats to take away sins. Only the priests were allowed in the Holy Place. No one but the high priest was allowed in the Holy of holies and that was once a year on the Day of Atonement.[41]

As the prophet Jeremiah foretold,[42] God initiated a new covenant: "I will put my laws in their hearts, and I will write them on their minds. I will remember their sins and their lawless deeds no more"[43] All of this was made possible by the blood of Jesus. He took our sins and nailed them to the cross. Therefore, "Where there is forgiveness of sins and lawless deeds, there is no longer any offering for sin."[44]

---

[41] Hebrews 9:1–7
[42] Jeremiah 31:33–35
[43] Hebrews 10:16–17
[44] Hebrews 10:18

Through the blood of Jesus, we have confidence to enter the sanctuary by the new and living way. With the tearing of the flesh of Jesus, a curtain was no longer needed. In the temple, the curtain or veil separated God's earthly presence in the Holy of holies from the people. It signified the sin which separated them from God. The curtain was torn from top to bottom when Jesus died on the cross.[45]

Through Christ's atonement, we are at-one-ment, no longer forbidden to be in God's presence; we are in and can enter in through the blood of Christ. Where there is forgiveness of sins and lawless deeds, there is no longer any offering for sin. For Christ also suffered for sins once for all, the righteous for the unrighteous, in order to bring us to God. He was put to death in the flesh, but made alive in the spirit.[46]

We can walk right up to God, full of confidence, knowing we are presentable. We have no need for a priest to intercede for us, to sacrifice on our behalf. Jesus did that. Because of this, we have a new and living way, a better way. No longer under the burden of the Law, we have been set free. We have a new life in Christ Jesus, one of faith, hope, and love.

Because of this new life in Christ, we can approach God with a true heart full of the assurance of our faith. Because of Christ, our hearts have been sprinkled clean from all sin. We place our faith in the Lord Jesus Christ when we believe in, trust in, rely on, and depend upon him.

Because of this new life we keep a grip on our confession of our unwavering hope found only in and through Christ Jesus. God is faithful. Christ is faithful. Therefore, our hope, what we know and can firmly state with conviction is God keeps his promise. It is God who has called us into fellowship with him through his only begotten son.

Because of this new life we must encourage one another to love, to serve, and to worship.

We love others through our service. We love God through our worship. We encourage one another through our community fellowship. As individuals we practice every day what was learned as a group.

After all, it really is a wonderful life.

---

[45] Mark 15:37–38
[46] 1 Peter 3:18

STEPPING
INTO
EASTER

	Easter Year B John 20:1–18 Why Are You Weeping?	
I'm a crier, so I understand Mary crying. Jesus was many things to her: he was healer, teacher, master, and friend.	Mary didn't recognize Jesus until she heard his voice. She had spent lots of time with Jesus, and she knew that voice (John 10:27).	We must have a strong foundation of scripture, a strong relationship with Jesus, and a strong communication system with God.
Mary had heard him teach love and forgiveness and saw him heal others. Jesus was her hope, and now her hope was gone.	It was the voice of hope, of love, the voice that meant everything to her.	We must know scripture so we can stand firm. We must know God personally so we will recognize his voice. We must pray without ceasing.
Doctrine was the furthest thing from her heart. Her heart was broken. In a blink of an eye, her world changed.	Mary Magdalene wanted to cling to Jesus, hold on to him, and not allow him to get away from her again. This is what we can learn from Mary Magdalene.	Jesus knows why we are standing at the tomb weeping. When he calls our name, we must turn around, for there is our hope.
Are you standing by the tomb crying? It could be the tomb of a loved one, a broken marriage, financial ruin, unrealized dream, or depression.		Hear the good news. He still removes stones from our empty tombs. Christ is risen. He has risen indeed!

Easter Year B
Why Are You Weeping?
John 20:1–18

Being a crier myself, I understand why Mary Magdalene was weeping. The One who healed her was nowhere to be found. Since that day she had closely followed Jesus. She heard him teach about love and forgiveness. She saw him heal others as he had healed her. He was her hope and now he was gone, and so was her hope. She was probably remembering all the times they had spent together, the times he made her feel so special. Doctrine was the farthest thing from her heart. Her heart was broken. In a blink of an eye her world had changed. She would miss spending time with Jesus; he was taken too soon.

Are you standing by the tomb weeping? Maybe it's the tomb of a loved one, or the tomb of a broken marriage or the tomb of financial ruin, or the tomb of an unrealized dream or maybe the tomb of depression.

When we are standing at the tomb we feel hopeless, unlovable, alone, vulnerable, and as if we are sitting in total darkness. Standing by the tomb we fill empty. Probably a lot of the same things Mary Magdalene felt that day standing at the tomb.

Mary Magdalene didn't know it was Jesus until he spoke her name. That voice! She knew that voice![47] That was the voice of hope; it was love, it was everything to her, and it was all she needed. She then knew it was Jesus and the first thing she wanted to do was to

---

[47] John 20:27

cling to him; hold on to him and not allow him to get away from her again. Mary Magdalene had spent so much time with Jesus she recognized him by his voice.

In our lives we will face many empty tombs. We will feel lost and unsure of what we should do. In order to face these times with hope, the hope of our calling, we must have a good solid foundation of Scripture, a good solid relationship with the Lord, and a good solid communication system.

We must know the word of God and where we can go to find encouragement, hope, peace, understanding, empathy, and sympathy. We will need scripture to stand firm against what makes us stand by the tomb weeping.

We must have a good solid relationship with the Lord. We must know him on a personal, intimate level. We must have a past with Jesus in order to have a future. We must be able to recall all the times Jesus has asked us why we are crying and how he was faithful.

We must have a good solid communication system between us and God so we need to develop the habit of praying without ceasing. We should talk with God throughout our day and wait and listen to what he has to say to us. Once we know Jesus's voice, we will be able to distinguish it from all the other voices in our heads including our own. Jesus knows why we are standing at the tomb weeping. When he calls our name, we must turn around for there is our hope.

The good news is God still rolls away the stone of the tombs of our lives.

When we think God is nowhere because in our pain we do not see or recognize him, that is the time to know that God is now here.

Hear the good news!

Christ has risen! The tomb is empty!

He has risen indeed!

	Easter 2 Year B John 20:19–29 A Room Full of Doubters	
What words come to mind when I say Peter? If I said Matthew or John? What if I said Thomas?	We learn from scripture Jesus did not blame the disciples for not believing. He did not condemn them for their lack of faith (John 3:17, Rom. 8:1).	Mary Magdalene was not allowed to touch Jesus. But she believed because she recognized the voice of Jesus.
Why do we remember the negative about Thomas? Maybe it helps us with our own disbelief.	Alfred L. Tennyson— "There lives more faith in honest doubt than in half the creeds." Doubt brings about open and honest communication.	The disciples in a locked room believe when they saw Jesus's scars. Thomas believed when he saw and touched the scars of Jesus.
Disciples in a locked room, scared of the Jews, feared for their lives. A lack of faith is fear.	Jesus used this opportunity for a faith lesson, a little show-and-tell. Jesus showed his scars to the disciples in the locked room and they believed.	We are all at different faith levels. Jesus will meet us on whatever level we find ourselves and help our unbelief.
The disciples doubted as much as Thomas. They only believed when Jesus showed them his scars.	Jesus told Thomas to place his finger in the scars on his hands and side. Then Thomas believed.	Jesus told Thomas not to doubt but to believe. Same thing to us. Faith is not the absence of doubt. It is overcoming doubt. Learn to be honest with God.
The disciples tell Thomas, "We have seen the Lord." Same words of Mary Magdalene when she encountered Jesus at the tomb.		

Easter 2 Year B
Seeing Is Believing
John 20:19–29

What words come to mind when I say Peter? What about Matthew or John? What if I said Thomas? Most of us would say doubter. Why do we remember the negative about Thomas? Maybe it helps us with our own disbelief.

If we look again at scripture, we find a room full of doubters. We find the apostles in a locked room, scared of the Jews. They feared for their lives even though they had heard Jesus ask the Father to protect them when he was gone.[48] A lack of faith is fear. However, once Jesus showed them his scars, they believed.

Thomas was absent that day, but when he returned, the other disciples told him, "We have seen the Lord." These are the same words Mary Magdalene spoke to them after she had returned from the empty tomb and her encounter with Jesus.

When the two on the Road to Emmaus told the disciples they had seen and been with the Lord, they did not believe and were asking the two questions when Jesus appeared.[49] They had been told three times of seeing Jesus, so they doubted just as much if not more than Thomas.

What we learn about being a doubter is Jesus didn't blame the disciples for not believing. He did not condemn the disciples for

---

[48] John 17
[49] Luke 24:44–53

their lack of faith.[50] Alfred Lord Tennyson said, "There lives more faith in honest doubt than in half the creeds." Doubt brings about open and honest communication between us and the Lord.

Jesus used the opportunity for a faith lesson. It was show-and-tell time. He greeted those in the locked room with, "Peace be with you." Then he showed his scars to the disciples and repeated, "Peace be with you." This was when the disciples believed. Jesus is able to turn out doubts to beliefs and our fear into peace.

With Thomas Jesus let him place his finger in the scars on his hands and let him touch his side. This is what Thomas needed to do in order to believe. Mary Magdalene was not allowed to hold on to Jesus, but she believed because she heard and recognized his voice. The other disciples had to see the scars to believe. We are all at different faith levels. Do not shame a follower for the level of faith they have. Jesus will meet us on whatever level and help our unbelief. Jesus told Thomas not to doubt but to believe. He says the same thing to us.

Doubt is the bedrock of honesty. Faith is not the absence of doubt. It is overcoming doubt. We must learn to be honest with God.

---

[50] John 3:17, Romans 8:1

	Easter 3 Year B Luke 24:36b–48 See Me, Touch Me	
Prior to our scripture, we have the two disciples on the Road to Emmaus to whom Jesus appeared. They recognized Jesus in the breaking of the bread.	Apostles, while in their joy, were disbelieving and still wondering even after he appealed to their senses.	To see and touch God, we must have acts of mercy.
These two go and tell the eleven, we have seen the Lord. This is the same thing Mary Magdalene told the apostles.	How can we see and touch God every day?	Feed the hungry Give drink to the thirsty Welcome a stranger Clothe the naked Care for the sick Visit the imprisoned
Jesus appears to the eleven apostles who were startled and frightened. He asked why are you frightened and why do doubts arise in your hearts?	To see and touch God we must have acts of piety.	Just as you did it to one of the least of these who are members my family, you did it to me.
Jesus appeals to their senses. The sense of sight; see my hands and feet. Sense of touch. Touch my flesh and bones.	Daily prayer and praise Daily reading of Scripture Daily meditating on Scripture Daily journaling and worshipping Partaking of Communion	The more we see Jesus, the more we touch Jesus, and the more we believe.

Easter 3 Year B
See Me Touch Me
Luke 24:36b–48

Prior to our scripture reading for today, we have the two disciples on the Road to Emmaus to whom Jesus appeared. They did not recognize Jesus. They had hoped, but it was already the third day. Jesus did not reveal himself until he shared the breaking of bread. Then he explained the scriptures to them.

These two disciples go and tell the eleven disciples, "We have seen the Lord." This is the same thing Mary Magdalene told the apostles. Jesus appears to the eleven who were startled and frightened. He asked, "Why are you frightened and why do doubts arise in your hearts?"

Jesus appeals to their senses. The sense of sight: see my hands and feet. The sense of touch: touch my flesh and bones. Only after they saw did they believe it was Jesus. Scripture tells us that the apostles while in their joy were disbelieving and still wondering.

How can we see and touch God every day? To see and touch God, we must have acts of piety. These include but not limited to daily prayer and praise, daily reading of scripture, daily meditating on scripture, daily journaling and worshipping and the partaking of Communion. Though these disciplines we develop a relationship with Christ and we develop sensitive hearing so we are able to know when he speaks to our spirit.

To see and touch God, we must have acts of mercy. We are taught to feed the hungry, give drink to the thirsty, welcome the stranger, clothe the naked, care for the sick, visit those in prison.

Jesus tells us doing these things to the least of these who are members of his family, we have done it to him.

Are we able to see Jesus in the face of the homeless or the face of the hungry and thirsty? Will we welcome the stranger into our home and see to any or all of their needs? Will we clothe dirty naked people? Will we care for the sick and visit those in prison? Are we able to do these things without passing judgment? Are we able to do it over and over again?

We are the hands and feet of Christ. If we will step out of our comfort zone and treat those less fortunate than ourselves with dignity, mercy, grace, and love, we will surely see and touch not only Jesus, but the face of God.

	Easter 4 Year B John 10:11–18 It's All about Relationship	
Rural Ireland has common flock, and sheep are color-coded and sorted for ownership. Jesus doesn't need a system because with us he has a relationship.	The good shepherd lays down his life for his sheep. Shepherd would literally lay down across the gate opening in order to protect his sheep.	Ezekiel 34 compares bad shepherd or false prophets with a good shepherd.
Jesus compares his relationship with us to a good shepherd and his sheep. He knows our voice and we are to know his voice.	Jesus laid down his life for us of his own free will. No one took it from him. Jesus gave up his will in order to do God's will.	The true shepherd searches for his sheep and rescues them from places scattered. On days of cloud and darkness, feeds with good pasture.
In Greek, good means beautiful as an outward sign of an inward good, noble, honorable character. Know means to know, especially through personal experience.	The good shepherd takes care of his sheep. Jesus takes care of us. He provides all we need. In turn we are to take care of others.	The true shepherd allows rest in lush green fields. He seeks the lost and brings back the strayed, binds up the injured, strengthens the weak, and feeds them justice.
We should be familiar with Jesus's voice so we can distinguish it from any other voice, especially our own.		Isaiah 61:1 Psalm 23 rewrite
To hear the voice of Jesus is a sign or mark of faithfulness to him and his word. It shows we are part of the flock.		

Easter 4 Year B
It's All about Relationship
John 10:11–18

In rural Ireland they have what is called common flock. More than one farmer uses the same land to graze their sheep. To designate ownership, the sheep are color-coded. A splashes of different colors are painted on the sheep's coat. At sheering time each farmer will know which sheep belongs to them based on this coloring system. The good Shepherd doesn't need any system because what he has with us is a relationship.

Jesus makes an analogy of his relationship with us as to a shepherd and his sheep. Jesus says he is the good Shepherd. The Greek word for *good* means beautiful, as an outward sign of the inward good, noble, honorable character.[51] Jesus further states he knows his own and his own know him. The Greek word for *know* means to know, especially through personal experience.[52] Well-trained sheep will only respond to their shepherd's voice. There is a relationship between the shepherd and his sheep. So it should be with us and God. We should be so familiar with Jesus's voice that we can distinguish it from any other voice, especially our own. To hear the voice of Jesus is a sign or mark of faithfulness to him and his word. It shows we are part of the flock.

The good shepherd lays down his life for his sheep. In the book *A Shepherd Looks at Psalm 23*, Philip Keller tells that at night, the

---

[51] 2570 Strong's
[52] 1970 Strong's

shepherd would literally lay down across the gate opening so that no sheep would get out without him knowing it and the shepherd could ward off any predators who tried to get to the sheep. Jesus laid down his life of his own free will and in obedience to God. He even states that no one took it from him. He gave up his will for God's will.

Just as the good shepherd takes care of his sheep, Jesus takes care of us. He provides all we need. In turn we are to take care of others. We are to feed the hungry, care for the sick, clothe the naked, visit those in prison. Jesus takes care of us so that we can be in ministry for him and to him. As we have done to the least of these, my family, you have done it to me.[53]

In the thirty-fourth chapter of Ezekiel, the bad shepherd or false prophets are compared with the good shepherd. The true shepherd searches for his sheep and rescues them from places scattered to on days of cloud and darkness. He feeds with good pasture and allows them to rest in lush green fields. The true shepherd will seek the lost and bring back the strayed, bind up the injured, strengthen the weak, and he will feed them justice.[54] "The spirit of the Lord God is upon me, because the Lord has anointed me; he has sent me to bring good news to the oppressed, to bind up the brokenhearted, to proclaim liberty to the captives and release to the prisoners."[55]

These passages from Ezekiel and Isaiah reminds me of Psalm 23. I took liberty with it and personalized it.

My Psalm 23

The Lord is my good Shepherd. He calls me away when I need rest. He calms the storm before he leads me to the still waters.
He restores my soul and I have peace.
No matter what lies ahead, I will be of great joy. I will have no fear because the Lord is always with me.
Prayer and scripture comfort me.

---

[53] Matthew 25:40
[54] Ezekiel 34:11–16
[55] Isaiah 61:1

The good Shepherd anoints me, and all my enemies can do is watch. I am richly blessed.

Grace and mercy follows me wherever I go because I go where the Good Shepherd leads me.[56]

The Good Shepherd, through his life and death, guaranteed my eternal home and there I will abide.

Jesus is faithful. We can depend on him for all our needs. But we also need a personal relationship with him, one where we spend time reading his word, talking with him and listening to him. Then we will learn his voice and he will lead us on the right path.

---

[56] Written by Lillith O'Shann Edmiston Moore. Do not use without permission.

	Easter 5 Year B John 15:1–8 Naked Fruit? No Bear Fruit!	
Dormant—prevents buds opening prematurely, just the right amount of pruning. God watches closely to know the proper time for our pruning.	Blossoming—plants have different parts with an equal purpose and importance. We each have a gift that is needed for the body of Christ, the church.	Ripening—hand thinning to produce better fruit and keep branches from breaking. We have a hands-on God (Jer. 18).
God removes every branch in Christ who does not produce fruit. To remove, lift upon oneself, and carry what has been raised. God raises us up so we may bear fruit.	Pollination during this stage. Transfer pollen within the plant cross-pollination with other plants.	Chemicals are applied to prevent and control diseases to have blemish-free marketable fruit.
God prunes those bearing fruit. In verse 3 the word cleansed is the same as pruned (Heb. 4:12).	We transfer the word of God within ourselves through prayer and study. We are a connectional church and we must cross-pollinate with others so we will grow.	Our chemical is the blood of Christ. We are reconciled by Christ's death so we will be holy in God's sight without blemish.
Budding—thirteen distinct stages of growth. Farmer knows stages so he can know if there is growth. We must test ourselves to see if we are still growing in Christ.		Harvest, end of the growing season. If you're breathing it's not your harvest time. Get ready to be pruned and blossom and produce fruit that will last.
Homemade biscuits. Don't get cooked in the squat. Make sure you rise to your potential.		

Easter 5 Year B
Naked Fruit? No! Bear Fruit!
John 15:1–8

God is the vine grower. Jesus is the vine. We are the branches. The life cycle of a fruit tree is similar to our own. Just like fruit trees, we too go through stages of development and change as we become mature followers of Christ.

The first stage of a fruit tree is dormant. During this stage the tree is watched closely to ensure no premature budding. This also requires just the right amount of pruning at the right time. God watches us closely to see we do not prematurely run ahead of him usually guessing what we are to do. He prunes as needed, and it seems we need a lot of pruning!

God removes every branch in Christ who does not produce fruit. This does not mean he lops us off and cast us aside. The word to remove means to lift upon oneself and carry what has been raised. God raises us up so we may bear fruit. As the song says, "You raise me up so I can stand on mountains. You raise me up to walk on stormy seas. I am strong when I am on your shoulders. You raise me up to more than I can be."[57] Only when God raises us up from the ground can we be more and do more.

The fruit tree must be pruned during the dormant stage. This produces new growth. God prunes every branch bearing fruit. We are cleansed by the word of Jesus. The word for cleansed is the same word for prune. "Indeed, the word of God is living and active, sharper than

---

[57] "You Raise Me Up"

any two-edged sword, piercing until it divides soul from spirit, joints from marrow; it is able to judge the thoughts and intentions of the heart."[58] Now that is pruning.

The next stage is budding. There are thirteen distinct stages of growth. The farmer must know all of these stages to see if the fruit is growing. "Examine yourselves to see whether you are living in the faith. Test yourselves. Do you not realize that Jesus Christ is in you?—Unless, indeed, you fail to meet the test!"[59] Have you ever cooked homemade biscuits? They start to rise and then just stop. They get cooked in the squat. We need to examine ourselves to see if we got cooked in the squat instead of rising to our potential.

Next is blossoming stage. Plants have different parts and purposes and all are needed. One is not more important than the other. During this stage plants will transfer seeds within the plant. They also must cross-pollinate where the pollen is transferred to another plant and produces stronger plants. God has given us different spiritual gifts. One gift is not greater than the other but all are needed.[60] We must transfer the word of God within us so that we will grow and blossom. We are also a connectional church and we must cross-pollinate with others so we will grow stronger.

The next stage is ripening. This requires hand thinning to produce better fruit and keep the limbs from breaking. In Jeremiah 18 we read about the potter reworking the clay until he reaches the desired outcome. We have a hands-on God. He must stay very close to us, shaping us until we ripen into his image.

During this stage, chemicals are applied to prevent and control pest and diseases to have blemish-free marketable fruit. Our chemical is the blood of Christ. We are reconciled by Christ's death so we will be holy in God's sight without blemish.[61]

The final stage is harvest, the end of the growing season. If you are still breathing, it is not your harvest time. Get ready for some pruning so you may blossom, ripen, and produce fruit for God that will last.

---

[58] Hebrews 4:12
[59] 2 Corinthians 13:5
[60] 1 Corinthians 12
[61] Colossians 1:22

	Easter 6 Year B John 15:9–17 Abide	
Tell my dog to stay and she follows me. Tell her again and she stays. Doing what I said. She stays or remains with me.	We are to talk with him, not to him, and we are to give him time to answer. We are to read, study, and meditate on scripture.	Enables us to love one another as Jesus loves. No greater love when a friend lays down his life for a friend.
Jesus says to abide in his love. Abide is dwell, remain, stay in a given place, state, or relation.	What happens when we abide? Enables us to have Jesus complete joy in us.	Love—agape. Affection, good will, love from Christian to Christian, love going forth from your soul and taking up abode in others.
Remain in his love is to embrace God's will. Choosing from his choices and obeying them through his power.	"The joy of the Lord is my strength" (Neh. 8:10). Rejoice hard times. Corrie ten Boom rejoiced over fleas.	Lay down life, lay down or to bend downward. Life—the human soul, soul as the seat of affection and will.
The branch receives nourishment through the vine. We receive God's word through Jesus Christ. We feed on his word.	Enables us to keep Jesus's commandments and be considered as friends.	Enables us to bear fruit that will last. We were chosen and appointed to bear fruit.
We must stay connected to Jesus through acts of piety and perpetual prayer, where we are aware of Jesus 24-7.	We are called friends because Jesus has made known to us everything he has heard from the Father.	Bear fruit by actively doing what God prefers with him by his power and direction. This can only be done through abiding.

Easter 6 Year B
Abide
John 15:9–17

Do you know what my little dog does when I say stay? She follows me. So I try again. Stay, while pointing my finger. She still follows me. I've decided she is doing exactly what I've said. She stays with me wherever I go. She is abiding.

Jesus says we are to abide in his love. To abide is to dwell, remain, or stay in a given place, state, or relation. The word love, agapao (ag-ap-ah'-o), means to embrace God's will, choosing his choices, and obeying them through his power. In order to do the will of God, we must develop the practice of piety. This involves reading and meditating on God's word and praying without ceasing. These will help us know God's will and enable us to keep his commandments. Jesus abides in God's love because he was obedient. We are to do the same.

Just as the branch receives nourishment from the vine we receive our nutrients from God's word through Jesus Christ. Through scripture we receive the word of God which feeds us. When we meditate on his word we learn to discern the will of God for our lives. We need to be familiar with scripture so we won't believe just anything someone tells us. We need to know scripture so we are able to battle Satan as Jesus did in the wilderness.

What happens when we abide in his love?

It enables us to have Jesus's joy completed in us. We may not always be happy but we should always have joy in Christ. Nehemiah 8:10 states, "The joy of the Lord is my strength." Even in times of darkness, we should have joy. Corrie ten Boom along with members of her family helped many Jews escape the Nazi's death camps. Imprisoned for their actions, Corrie and her family awaited death. They lived in horrible living conditions including fleas. Corrie and her sister were thankful for the fleas because the guards would not come into the room and they were able to read the Bible and teach others God's word. They rejoiced in having fleas.[62]

When we abide in Jesus's love we are enabled to keep God's commandments, and we are considered his friends. Being friends with Jesus, we are informed of all things the Father has told Jesus.

We are enabled to love one another as Jesus loves. "No one has greater love than this, to lay down one's life for one's friends." Love, agape (ag-ah-pay), is affection, good will, love from Christian to Christian, love going forth from your soul and taking up abode in others.

We are enabled to bear fruit that last. God has equipped us with certain gifts we are to use for building up the body of Christ. With our gifts and Jesus's power, we are able to bear fruit. God chooses us and what we are to do. We don't get to choose. We give up our will for God's will.

We bear fruit by actively doing what God prefers with him and by his power and direction. This can only be done through a personal relationship and abiding with God the Father, Jesus the Son, and the Holy Spirit.

---

[62] *The Hiding Place* by Corrie ten Boom

	Ascension Day Year B Luke 24:44–53 Parting Gifts	
When friends leave, we have a party and give parting gifts. There is joy with an underlying sadness similar to what the disciples must have felt.	The gift of understanding. He opened their minds to the Law of Moses, prophets, and psalms.	We shall mount up with wings like eagles. This is upward strength we receive by worshipping Jesus and blessing God.
Since his death, Jesus had appeared several time to his disciples. Empty tomb. Road to Emmaus, Upper Room	The gift of fulfilled prophecy. Messiah must suffer, rise on third day from the dead, repentance and forgiveness of sins proclaimed to all nations.	We shall run and not be weary. This is outward strength we receive from other believers. Other believers provide encouragement and strength.
Now he would disappear, be taken from their sight again, but this time before leaving, he gave them parting gifts.	The gift of hope. Jesus promised the disciples the Holy Spirit. But now they were to tarry in Jerusalem until they received the Holy Spirit.	We shall walk and not faint. This is outward strength. Walk the walk and talk the talk. Keep the mission. No retirement age or plan. Other will see our mission.
	Are we good at waiting on the Lord? Things happen when we do.	The ascension is the bridge between the ministry of Jesus and the mission of the church. The Holy Spirit is the agent toward the fulfillment of God's mission.
	We shall renew our strength. Inner strength we receive through prayer.	Because Jesus ascended, we have the parting gift of the Holy Spirit; the gift that keeps on giving.

Ascension Day Year B
Parting Gifts
Luke 24:44–53

When close friends are about to leave us, we give them something to help them remember us. There is usually a party with great joy but with an underlying sadness. I'm sure this was also the case with the disciples as they say so long for now to Jesus.

Since his death, Jesus had appeared several times to his disciples. He had appeared to Mary Magdalene and the other women at the empty tomb. He appeared to the two disciples on the Road to Emmaus. He appeared to the disciples in the upper room and again in the upper room when Thomas was present. Now he would disappear, be taken from their sight again. But this time, before leaving them, Jesus gave them parting gifts.

One gift was the gift of understanding. He opened their minds to the Law of Moses, prophets, and psalms. It is said that the wife of Albert Einstein was once asked if she understood her husband's theory of relativity. She replied, "No, but I know my husband and that's enough."[63] When we are reading scripture, we should ask Jesus to open our minds and grant us wisdom so that we may understand what he is saying to us.

Another gift was the fulfillment of prophecy. Jesus explained that it was written the Messiah must suffer, rise on the third day from the dead, and repentance and forgiveness of sins proclaimed to all nations beginning with Jerusalem. The disciples had been witnesses

---

[63] sermons.org

to these things. This is more proof for them that Jesus is the Messiah and that is based on scripture, Old Testament teachings.

Another gift was a gift of hope. Jesus promised the disciples the Holy Spirit. But for now, they were to tarry in Jerusalem until they were clothed with power from on high.[64] The word tarry means to abide or stay in one place. The word abide should ring a bell from the reading of John 15, the story of the vine grower, the vine, and the branches. So what did the disciples do while they were abiding? When they returned to Jerusalem, all of them constantly devoted themselves to prayer.[65]

Are you good at tarrying or waiting on the Lord? We think we are until we have to do it. But scripture tells us about those who wait on the Lord.

They shall renew their strength. This is the inner strength we received when we devote ourselves to prayer. Prayer keeps us connected to the Trinity and helps us conquer and recover from life's hurdles that appear before us.

They shall mount up with wings like eagles. This is upward strength that we receive through worship. Worshipping Christ and blessing God brings us great joy. We are to move upward; we must remember the joy of the Lord is our strength.[66] God will provide you with whatever you need to accomplish great heights for his glory.

They shall run and not be weary, which is outward strength. We must run the race of endurance that is before us.[67] Too often we try to run someone else's race. We must run the race of endurance with the help of all fellow Christians, those you believe in and follow Jesus. With their encouragement and support, they will help us get a firm grip on our calling as we wait upon the Lord.

They shall walk and not faint, which is onward strength. We walk the walk and talk the talk. There is no retirement age or plan. We are to keep going, keep fulfilling the mission. Our mission is the

---

[64] Acts 1:8, Luke 24:49
[65] Acts 1:14
[66] Nehemiah 8:10
[67] Hebrews 12:1

same as the one Jesus gave to the disciples. Others will see our out-ward actions and respond. We are to continue onward.

"The ascension is the bridge between the ministry of Jesus and the mission of the church. Because Jesus ascended, the Holy Spirit could descend upon the church. The Holy Spirit is the active agent toward the fulfillment of God's mission."[68] Because Jesus ascended, we have received a parting gift of the Holy Spirit. The gift that keeps on giving.

---

[68] sermons.org

Easter 7 Year B
John 17:6–19
Protect and Serve

The time was drawing near. Jesus had completed his mission. One more prophecy to fulfill.

Jesus had selected this small group from the world, but they were no longer in the world. There had been a change, a transformation.

Jesus looked up to heaven. Worry looks around; faith looks up.

Jesus had washed his disciples' feet, talked of his betrayal, gave a new commandment to love one another, and promised the Holy Spirit.

Jesus would no longer be in the world, so he prayed these things for his then disciples and for future ones.

Jesus prayed for his followers, not the world. Jesus was concerned with those who had changed, transformed, but still had to live in the world.

Jesus prayed for protection so there would be community. His desire was to have unity in community.

Jesus prayed for protection from the evil one. He was not asking for isolation but insulation. Protection would be needed as the disciples were in ministry.

Jesus prayed for sanctification. God's word is truth. Scripture changes us.

Jesus prayed so we might serve.

Easter 7 Year B
Protect and Serve
John 17:6–19

The time was drawing near. Jesus knew that the hour had come. He had completed his life-giving mission. There was one more prophecy to fulfill.

Jesus had washed the disciples' feet teaching them to be a servant. He had told them about his betrayal by one of them and gave them a new commandment to love one another as he had loved them. He promised the Holy Spirit and told them how to abide and many other teachings. But now the hour had come.

Jesus had selected this small group from the world but they were no longer of the world. There had been a change, a transformation. They had been witnesses to the miracles Jesus performed and had been protected by the power of his name. They were not the same people as they were when they were called to be a follower of Christ.

Jesus would no longer be in the world for he was going to the Father. So he prayed for the following things for those disciples and for us. Yes, we were on Jesus's mind as he was about to face death. Jesus looked up at the heavens and began to pray for his disciples and for the disciples that would follow.

First thing we should notice, Jesus looked up to heaven. Worry looks around. Faith looks up. We have a tendency to bow our head in prayer. What if we looked up, with eyes open expecting to see and feel God's presence as we talk with him?

Jesus prayed for his followers, not the world. Jesus loves everyone but he was concerned with those who had been changed, transformed, but still had to live in this world.

Jesus prayed for protection so there would be a community, a community of one mind and of one accord. He desired unity in the community and relationships such as God the Father, God the Son, and God the Holy Spirit enjoyed. Jesus prayed for his joy to be complete in his disciples.

Jesus prayed for protection from the evil one. While Jesus was with the disciples, he protected them and guarded them, but he was leaving and he asked for their protection in his name. Jesus was not asking the Father to isolate but to insulate his followers. He did not want his disciples to be taken out of the world but protection as long as they were in this world. Each disciple has a special gift they are to use in ministry to the Lord. Discipleship is not a detour around the world but a certain path through the world. He knew protection would be needed as his followers walked their own path of ministry.

Jesus prayed for his disciples to be sanctified in truth, which is God's Word. If we are a disciple of Christ's, we are pupils, learners, seekers of truth who learn the doctrines of Scripture and the lifestyle they require. A disciple of Christ is not just a student of the word but one who changes their way of living. Reading God's word daily changes us. It molds us. We begin to start looking and acting more like Jesus and less like ourselves. Transformation takes place.

Jesus prayed so that we might serve. An encounter with Jesus demands a change and an action. We learn to be like Jesus and we change. We learn what servant means, what ministry means, and we are compelled to change the world just as we have changed.

STEPPING
INTO
PENTECOST

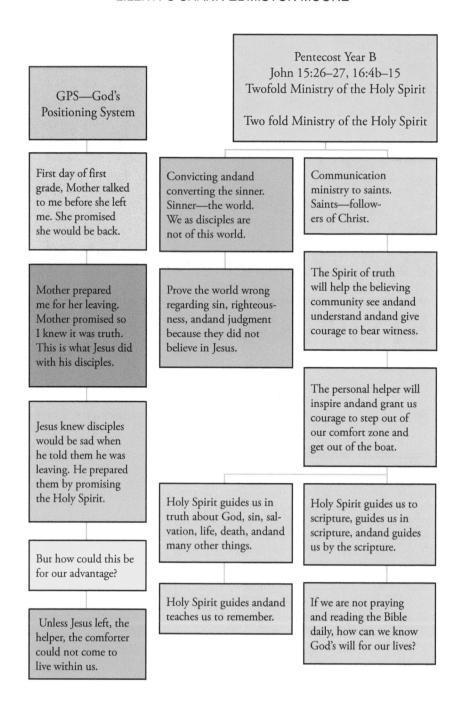

Pentecost Year B
John 15:26–27, 16:4b–15
Twofold Ministry of the Holy Spirit

Two fold Ministry of the Holy Spirit

GPS—God's
Positioning System

First day of first
grade, Mother talked
to me before she left
me. She promised
she would be back.

Convicting andand
converting the sinner.
Sinner—the world.
We as disciples are
not of this world.

Communication
ministry to saints.
Saints—follow-
ers of Christ.

Mother prepared
me for her leaving.
Mother promised so
I knew it was truth.
This is what Jesus did
with his disciples.

Prove the world wrong
regarding sin, righteous-
ness, andand judgment
because they did not
believe in Jesus.

The Spirit of truth
will help the believing
community see andand
understand andand give
courage to bear witness.

The personal helper will
inspire andand grant us
courage to step out of
our comfort zone and
get out of the boat.

Jesus knew disciples
would be sad when
he told them he was
leaving. He prepared
them by promising
the Holy Spirit.

Holy Spirit guides us in
truth about God, sin, salvation, life, death, andand
many other things.

Holy Spirit guides us to
scripture, guides us in
scripture, andand guides
us by the scripture.

But how could this be
for our advantage?

Holy Spirit guides andand
teaches us to remember.

If we are not praying
and reading the Bible
daily, how can we know
God's will for our lives?

Unless Jesus left, the
helper, the comforter
could not come to
live within us.

Pentecost Year B
Twofold Ministry of the Holy Spirit
John 15:26–27, 16:4b–15

On my first day of first grade, my mother took me to school and left me. She had told me she would come back to get me and gave me instructions on how to behave. I'm pretty sure I was scared and lonely, but Momma returned like she said.

Before Mother died, she prepared me for her leaving and also gave me final instructions before she slipped into a coma. I was lonely and I was scared. I didn't want Momma to leave, but she would no longer be in pain if she went. I was torn.

Jesus knew the disciples were sad when he told them he was leaving. He prepared them for this by promising the power and presence of the Holy Spirit and gave them the ministry to testify about him. Jesus refers to the Holy Spirit as Advocate and the Spirit of truth. Other translations call him Personal Helper and Comforter. There are specific roles assigned to the Holy Spirit.

The Holy Spirit will be Jesus's presence in the unbelieving community and in the individual followers.

The Holy Spirit convicts and converts the world, the unbelievers. The Advocate, the Spirit of truth testifies on behalf of Jesus and proves the world wrong about sin, righteousness, and judgment.

The truth-telling judge proves to the unbelieving community that they are wrong about sin.

Christ paid the full payment for all sin. Unbelievers failed to accept the full pardon. "Indeed, God did not send the Son into the world to condemn the world, but in order that the world might be saved through him. Those who believe in him are not condemned; but those who do not believe are condemned already, because they have not believed in the name of the only Son of God."[69]

As prosecuting attorney, he proves the world wrong about righteousness.

They failed to understand the nature of the cross and the need for the cross. The Father showed his acceptance of the sacrifice by emptying the tomb.

The Holy Spirit will prove his case for judgment. Satan was judged at the cross. The Holy Spirit convinces people of the coming judgment.

The Spirit of truth guides us into all the truth. The Holy Spirit is a truth-telling teacher who reveals what he hears from God. He will guide believers in all truths; truth about sin, salvation, and righteousness—all we need to be a complete follower of Christ Jesus. "All scripture is inspired by God and is useful for teaching, for reproof, for correction, and for training in righteousness, so that everyone who belongs to God may be proficient, equipped for every good work."[70]

The Holy Spirit declares to believers things to come. The Holy Spirit leads us and we are to follow. He speaks truth about the church.

> This is the reason that I Paul am a prisoner for Christ Jesus for the sake of you Gentiles—for surely you have already heard of the commission of God's grace that was given me for you, and how the mystery was made known to me by revelation, as I wrote above in a few words, a reading of which will enable you to perceive my under-standing of the mystery of Christ. In former generations this mystery was not made known to humankind, as it has now been revealed to his holy apostles and prophets by the Spirit: that is, the Gentiles have become fellow

---

[69] John 3: 18
[70] 2 Timothy 3:16–17

heirs, members of the same body, and sharers in
the promise in Christ Jesus through the gospel.
Of this gospel I have become a servant according
to the gift of God's grace that was given me by
the working of his power.[71]

The Spirit of truth glorifies God by making him known. From
disciples to apostles, to teaching and preaching, the Holy Spirit
enables us to step out of our comfort zone and be the hands and feet
and heart of Christ. He gives us the courage to do what we are called
to do through Jesus Christ.

The Holy Spirit works through us, guiding us so that we are
equipped to testify to others about Jesus Christ and him crucified.
The Spirit of truth will help the believing community see and understand and give courage to bear witness to an unbelieving world.

---

[71] Ephesian 3:1–7

	Pentecost 2 Year B Mark 2:23–3: 6 Keeping the Sabbath Holy	
Growing up went to my grandparents every Sunday. Don't you kids fight on Sunday.	The Pharisees watched to see if he would heal on a Sunday. Pharisees were watching, gathering evidence against Jesus.	We are to love God and neighbor. To help someone in need, in brokenness in pain, shows love and compassion.
Only conflicts over the Sabbath found in Mark's Gospel.	Pharisees were more concerned with the law than the intent of the law.	Jesus was grieved at the hardness of their hearts. We know God is a compassionate God and Jesus was full of compassion.
One Sunday walking through a field, Jesus's disciples gathered heads of grain to eat. Pharisees accused them of working on the Sabbath.	Pharisees were silent so Jesus couldn't condemn them… Jesus grieved at the hardness of their hearts.	Law stated to keep Sabbath a day of rest, holy, set apart. We have been set apart. To be holy is to have the mind of Christ and walk as he walked.
Jesus reminded them of David and his followers eating the consecrated bread of presence.	First time Sabbath is mentioned (Exod. 16:23). Sabbath—Solemn rest, a gift from God.	As children of God, we are supposed to be different, unique, set apart from the world. One way we do this is through our compassion
Later Jesus heals a man with a withered hand. Jesus asked, "Is it lawful to do good or harm on the Sabbath, to save life or to kill?"	The Lord consecrated and blessed the Sabbath (Exod. 20:11). Consecrated—to observe or pronounce as ceremonially or morally clean, set apart.	Sanctification—to become holy, set apart. Good works become a way of life, not an obligation.
	Keep Sabbaths as they are a sign between God and his people they have been sanctified (Exod. 31:12–13).	What would honor God more than helping a neighbor in Jesus's name? WWJD?

Pentecost 2 Year B
Keeping the Sabbath Holy
Mark 2:23—3:6

When I was growing up, my family went to my grandparents' every Sunday. On special occasions such as Easter, Thanksgiving, and Christmas, all my aunts, uncles, and cousins would gather in the small farmhouse to observe the holiday and the family. Some of my cousins were rather rowdy and the teasing would start, then hurt feelings occurred. Next came the yelling and screaming. From the kitchen, we would hear my grandmother's voice, "Don't you kids fight on Sunday." I guess if we wanted to fight, we would have to do it Monday through Saturday.

One Sabbath Jesus and his disciples were walking through a field and they gathered heads of grain to eat. Ripened grain can be eaten whole. Not only is it tasty, it is a good source of nourishment. The Pharisees accused Jesus and his disciples of working on the Sabbath. Plucking bits of grain from another's field for sustenance was permitted under Mosaic Law.[72] Jesus refuted their allegation by reminding them of David and his companions eating the consecrated bread of presence in the temple. He continued saying, "The Sabbath was made for humankind and not humankind for the Sabbath, so the Son of Man is lord even of the Sabbath."

Later Jesus entered the synagogue and healed a man's withered hand. Jesus was placing the intent of the Law above the written law itself. The Pharisees watched him intently, not to listen and learn but

---

[72] Deuteronomy 23–25

117

to gather evidence against Jesus. Jesus questions them by asking, "Is it lawful to do good or to do harm on the Sabbath, to save life or to kill?" The Pharisees remained silent as they knew Jesus would condemn them. The Pharisees were religious leaders who should have led the people in righteousness. Instead the Pharisees plotted with their enemy the Herodians to kill Jesus. The Herodians were Jews who supported Rome and the "Herod" rulers. But the Pharisees put their differences aside and joined forces in order to destroy a common foe, Jesus.

The first time Sabbath is mentioned in scripture is Exodus 16:23. The Sabbath is a solemn rest that is a gift from God. God created the world for six days, and on the seventh, he rested. The Lord consecrated and blessed the Sabbath.[73] Consecrated means to observe or pronounce as ceremonially or morally clean, set apart. Blessed means to kneel and implies the bending of the knee.

God said to keep the Sabbaths as they are a sign between God and his people that they have been sanctified.[74] We are to love God and neighbor. To help someone in need, in brokenness, in pain shows love and compassion. Our God is a compassionate God and Jesus in full of compassion.

To be sanctified is to become holy, set apart. Through the process, good works become a way of life, not an obligation.

The Law stated to keep the Sabbath a day of rest, holy, set apart. We have been set apart. We are to be different, unique, set apart from the world. One way we do this is through our compassion. What would honor God more than helping a neighbor in Jesus's name? What would Jesus do?

---

[73] Exodus 20:11
[74] Exodus 31:12–13

	Pentecost 3 Year B Mark 3:20–35 The Will of God	
For most of us, our identity is found in our family. Today's scripture may sound strange to us.	God speaks in the language we know best. Not through our ears but through our circumstances	God provides the Holy Spirit in us to help us do his will. We still have free choice and we can disregard the prompting of the Spirit.
When asked, Jesus said his mother and brothers were those who did the will of God.	Once the crisis arrives, we have to decide what we are to do. We find ourselves at a crossroads and what we do from that point forward is monumental.	In order to do God's will, we must have intimate knowledge intimate friendship by doing his will from our hearts.
Rejoice always, pray without ceasing, give thanks in all circumstances; for this is the will of God in Christ Jesus for you (1 Thess. 5:16–18).	We do the will of God to be part of Jesus's family.	We are friends of God when we do what he says.
Rejoice in hope, patient in suffering, and persevere in prayer (Rom. 12:12).	We do the will of God so that we will not be foolish but make smart choices and wise decisions.	The more time we spend talking with God and reading his word, the more we will know God's ways. We will learn to discern his voice over others and our own.
Most of us find it difficult to always rejoice and give thanks in all circumstances. We look at the surface but not below it.	We do the will of God so we can have all spiritual wisdom and understanding so that we may lead lives worthy of the Lord.	As we grow spiritually, we become more aware of God, so we don't ask what is his will because the thought of choosing another way will never occur to us.
		God guides us through the promptings of his Holy Spirit. We must be attentive and sensitive to these nudges, promptings, and warnings.

Pentecost 3 Year B
The Will of God
Mark 3:20–35

For most of us, our identity is found in our family. I was Robert and Lilith's youngest girl. I was Renee's younger sister. I was Mrs. Franklin's granddaughter. When I was growing up, each new boyfriend was asked the same questions by my parents, "Who are your parents?" So our focus scripture may seem very strange to us.

When asked, Jesus said his mother and brothers were those who did the will of God. It's hard to do the will of God when you don't know what it is. It takes knowing God's heart and discerning his will. In 1 Thessalonians 5:16–18 it states, "Rejoice always, pray without ceasing, give thanks in all circumstances; for this is the will of God in Christ Jesus for you." We are to rejoice in hope, patient in suffering, and persevere in prayer.[75] Most of us find it difficult to always rejoice and give thanks in all circumstances. Some of our circumstances are not very pleasant. We look at the surface of our circumstances and not below. God speaks in the language we know best, not through our ears but through our circumstances. Once the crisis arrives, we have to decide what we are to do. We find ourselves at a crossroads, and what we do from this point forward is monumental.

Why do the will of God? Our first response seems pretty obvious: to be part of Jesus's family. If we are to be part of the family, we must be obedient to God's will. There are other reasons found in scripture for us to do God's will.

---

[75] Romans 12:12

We do the will of God so that we will not be foolish.[76] If we follow the will of God, we will make smart choices and wise decisions. We do the will of God so we can be filled with the knowledge of God's will in all spiritual wisdom and understanding so that we may lead lives worthy of the Lord.[77] If we do the will of God we will always honor God and please him, we will continually do good for others, and we will learn to know and recognize God.

How can we do the will of God? Not only does God expect us to do his will, he provides the Holy Spirit in us to help us do it.[78] But we still have free choice and we can disregard the promptings of the Spirit. In order to do the will of God, we must have an intimate knowledge of God.[79] We also must have an intimate friendship with God by doing his will from our hearts.[80] We are friends of God if we do what he commands.[81]

The more time we spend talking with God and reading his word, the more we will learn the nature of God and be able to discern his voice above others and our own. As we grow spiritually, we become more and more aware of God so that we do not need to ask what his will is because the thought of choosing another way will never occur to us. God guides us through the promptings of his Holy Spirit. We must be attentive and sensitive to these nudges, promptings, and warnings.

---

[76] Ephesians 5:17
[77] Colossians 1:9–10
[78] Hebrews 13:20–21
[79] Romans 12:1–2, John 10:14
[80] Ephesians 6:5–6
[81] John 15:14–15

	Pentecost 4 Year B Mark 4:26–34 Transformation Power	
	The Mustard Seed Bracelet	
Jesus used parables for comparative examples. Most of them were difficult to understand. Jesus would later explain them to the disciples.	The common themes of these two parables are similar to the parable of the sower. They deal with the soil, the earth producing of itself, and growth.	Jesus had humble beginnings. Born in a stable among the animals, he brought nothing with him. He left it all behind.
Using seeds, he explains the kingdom of God	There is a transforming power in the earth. The sower doesn't understand nor can he control the power. He buries a seed and abracadabra! Up comes a plant.	His ministry had humble beginnings, but through the power of the Holy Spirit, the kingdom grows. This too is a mystery.
In the first parable, seed is scattered and over time sprouts and grows. This growth is a mystical, complex, intricate process with hidden power.	These three parables show the kingdom of God comes from a humble beginning to a comparably large result due to the power of the Holy Spirit.	It is the power of the Holy Spirit inside us which changes us little by little until we are transformed into a disciple of Christ. This too is a mystery.
In the parable of the mustard seed, Jesus teaches the growth of the tiniest seed into a tree growing to fifteen feet with many heavy branches.		
In these heavy branches, birds find rest and protection. This too is a mystery of how something so small could serve such a large purpose.		

Pentecost 4 Year B
Transformative Power
Mark 4:26–34

How many remember the mustard seed bracelets of the 1960s? They were a simple bracelet with just one charm, a round globe with a tiny mustard seed in some type of liquid causing the seed to float. I remember Momma getting me a mustard seed bracelet and telling me the story of the mustard seed and how a little faith, small as the mustard seed, could move mountains. I would sit and look at the bracelet and marvel at its size, or the lack thereof.

Jesus often used parables as a teaching method. The meaning not often clear, he would explain to the disciples in private. Sometimes the disciples still would not get the point Jesus was trying to make. We too often miss the mark and fail to get the point.

Using seed, Jesus explains the kingdom of God. In the parable of the growing seed, the seed is scattered, and over time the seed sprouts and grows. First the stalk appears, then the head and then the full grain in the head. The growth of seed into a plant is a mystery that man cannot easily explain. It is a mystical, complex, and intricate process with hidden power.

In the parable of the mustard seed, Jesus teaches about the growth of the tiniest seed into a tree, growing to fifteen feet with many heavy branches, where birds can go for protection and rest. This too is a mystery of how something so small could serve such a large purpose.

The common themes of these two parables are similar to the parable of the sower. They deal with the soil, the earth producing of itself, and growth. The good soil of the kingdom of God produces its fruit by its own eternal power. There is a transforming power in the earth. The sower doesn't understand nor can he control the power. He buries a seed and abracadabra! Up comes a plant!

These parables show the kingdom of God comes from a humble beginning to a comparably large result due to the power of the Holy Spirit. Being born in a lowly stable, Jesus had humble beginnings. His ministry began small and grew way out of proportion compared to the beginning and continues to grow. Through the power of the Holy Spirit, the kingdom grows and becomes a force to be reckoned with.

It is the power of the Holy Spirit inside us that molds us, shapes us, and transforms us from our humble beginnings to becoming a disciple of Christ. This too is a mystery. Let those who have ears hear and those who have eyes see.

	Pentecost 5 Year B Mark 4:35–41 Raging Storms of Life	
Jesus invited his apostles to get on a boat and go to other side, which was Gentile territory. Jesus was extending his ministry beyond the Jews.	Jesus asked why they were afraid and questioned their lack of faith. Jesus did not say there was no reason to be afraid (Ps. 112:7–8).	Jesus is our life jacket. He prepares us for whatever we will have to face (Isa. 43:2, Isa. 41:10).
Jesus left the crowd without dismissing them. But they didn't leave him as there were other boats that went with Jesus and his apostles.	Apostles were in awe. They had seen many cured, healed, and cleansed but first time they had personally experienced Jesus's power (Ps. 107:28–29).	Jesus is the anchor of our souls. He is our hope and keeps us firm and secure in any storm (Heb. 6:19a, Jer. 12:11, Rom. 8:28, Ps. 57:1).
Jesus was tired from teaching and healing. In his humanness, he laid down and went to sleep (Prov. 3:24, Ps. 4:8).	In this life we go through many storms, big and little—financial, marital, emotional, physical, doubt, and death. Lord, don't you care? Three things to remember	Jesus is our lifeboat and he will allow us to escape the storm. He will alter our course and we will escape the impending storm (Ps. 34:17, Ps. 32:7; NIV).
A violent storm arose. The Apostles were frightened. At least four seasoned fishermen were on board who had experienced storms on the open seas before.		Next time we see a storm on the horizon and our little boat is about to get swamped, remember these three things: Jesus can walk with us through the storm, he can stand with us through the storm, or he can provide a way out of the storm. All we have to do is trust.
Apostles woke Jesus with a question, "Teacher, do you not care that we are perishing?"		
Jesus got up, rebuked the wind, and instructed the sea to be still. The deity of Jesus had authority over nature so the wind stopped and there was dead calm.		

Pentecost 5 Year B
Raging Storms of Life
Mark 4:35–41

Jesus invited the disciples to go across to the other side. Jesus left the crowd without dismissing them. But they didn't leave him as there were other boats that went with Jesus and the apostles.

The other side was Gentile territory, which shows Jesus was extending his ministry beyond the Jews. To cross over to the other side, they had to travel eight miles across the lake. This does not seem like a difficult task, but the geographic layout of this area added difficulty to their journey. The lake was seven hundred feet below sea level and was surrounded with mountains that rise three to four thousand feet above sea level on the north, east, and west. This made the climate vary and a wind storm could appear at any moment. This is what Jesus and the disciples encountered that day.

Jesus was tired from teaching and healing the crowds. In his humanness, he laid down and went to sleep. The image of him sleeping shows trust in God. "I will both lie down and sleep in peace; for you alone, O Lord, make me lie down in safety."

When a violent storm rose, the apostles were frightened. There were at least four seasoned fishermen on board who had experienced this type of storm. But they awoke Jesus and questioned his concern about their safety. Jesus got up, rebuked the wind, and instructed the sea to be still. The deity of Jesus had authority over nature, so the wind stopped and there was dead calm. Jesus wanted to know why they were frightened and questioned their lack of faith. Jesus did not say there was no reason to be afraid, but their faith should have kept them calm and given them peace. The apostles were in awe. They had seen many cured, healed, and cleansed, but this time they personally experienced Jesus's power. "Then they cried to the Lord in their trouble, and he brought them out from their distress; he made the storm be still, and the waves of the sea were hushed."[82]

In this life we go through many storms, big and little. Could be financial, marital, emotional, physical, or spiritual. We find ourselves crying out, "Lord, don't you care?"

When we find ourselves in the storms of life, we need to remember three things.

Jesus is our life jacket. He prepares us for whatever we will have to face. "When you pass through the waters, I will be with you; and through the rivers, they shall not overwhelm you; when you walk through fire you shall not be burned, and the flame shall not consume you."[83]

Jesus is the anchor of our soul. He is our hope and keeps us firm and secure in any storm. "We have this hope, a sure and steadfast anchor of the soul, a hope that enters the inner shrine behind the curtain."[84]

Jesus is our lifeboat, and he will allow us to escape the storm. He will alter our course and we will escape the impending storm. "When the righteous cry for help, the Lord hears, and rescues them from all their troubles.[85] You are a hiding place for me; you preserve me from trouble; you surround me with glad cries of deliverance. Selah"[86]

Next time we see a storm on the horizon and our little boat is about to get swamped, remember these three things: Jesus can walk with us through the storm, he can stand with us through the storm, or he can provide a way out of the storm. All we have to do is trust.

---

[82] Psalm 107:28–29
[83] Isaiah 43:2
[84] Hebrews 6:19a
[85] Psalm 34:17
[86] Psalm 32:7

	Pentecost 6 Year B Mark 5:21–43 The Compassion of Jesus	
Before we can go forward, we need to go back to the Old Testament.	Someone touched his cloak and power went out to them. When asked who had touched him, the woman with hemorrhage for twelve years confessed it was she.	Two examples of Jesus's compassion. He has compassion for us. He took our sins upon himself, died, and rose again so that we would be in right.
Under the Law, a person was considered unclean if they touched someone with blood or discharge issue or a dead body (Lev. 15:7, Num. 19:11–12).	Woman with the hemorrhage had been in isolation for twelve years. She couldn't worship, couldn't interact with family, friends, or community.	Those who may need our attention the most may be the least visible. We should stop and notice those in need.
Under Law Jesus's compassion would have made him unclean (Num. 5:2).	But she had heard about Jesus, so with rock solid faith she weathered the crowd. Her faith placed in Jesus had made her well.	Just like Jesus, we must not only stop and assist someone, we need to develop a relationship with them, have a conversation with them.
Today's passage, Jesus had crossed back to the other side, which was Jewish territory.	Jesus continues to Jairus's home to find his daughter dead. Jesus took her hand and restored her life.	Before Jesus tended to the request of the well-known and respected synagogue leader, he stopped for the one with no name, the one in the background.
Jairus, the synagogue leader, asked Jesus to lay hands on his sick daughter. They both knew how this would be perceived, but Jesus went anyway.		If God interrupts our plans, stop and pay attention to what is happening. Be the instrument God uses to show compassion to the one who needs it most.

Pentecost 6 Year B
The Compassion of Jesus
Mark 5:21–43

Before we can go forward, we need to go back to the Old Testament. Under the Law, a person was considered unclean if they touched someone with blood or discharge issues or a dead body.[87]

In today's passage, Jesus had crossed back to the other side, which was Jewish territory. Jairus, the synagogue leader, asked Jesus to lay hands on his sick daughter. Jairus had faith Jesus would meet his need but thought it necessary for him to actually lay hands on her, to touch her. They both knew how this would be perceived, but Jesus went anyway. Under the Law, Jesus's acts of compassion would have made him unclean.[88]

A huge crowd was following Jesus. Someone touched his cloak and power went out of him to them. When asked who had touched him, the woman with the hemorrhage for twelve years confessed it was she. She had been in isolation for twelve years. She couldn't worship, couldn't interact with family, friends, or community. But she had heard about Jesus, so with rock solid faith in him, she weathered the crowd. Jesus commends her for her faith and told her she was healed and to go in peace. Her faith placed in Jesus had made her well.

Jesus continues to Jairus's home only to be told Jairus's twelve-year-old daughter had died. Jesus told Jairus not to be afraid but to

---

[87] Leviticus 15:7, Numbers 19:11–12
[88] Numbers 5:2

keep believing. There were many neighbors and friends there to support Jairus. Jesus allowed only her parents and Peter, James, and John to enter the room with him. Jesus took her hand and restored her to life. Jairus's great faith in Jesus had returned her to life.

These are two examples of Jesus's compassion. Jesus cures the sick on his way to raise the dead, a miracle within a miracle. He took time to seek out the person who had touched him. Jesus could feel the desperation in the woman's touch and the desperation in the voice of Jairus.

Before Jesus tended to the request of the well-known and respected synagogue leader, he stopped for the one with no name, the one in the background. Those who may need our attention the most may be the least visible. We should stop and notice those in need. Just like Jesus, we must not only stop and assist someone; we need to develop a relationship with them, by having a conversation with them.

Jesus has compassion for us. He took our sins upon himself so that we would be in right relationship with God. He who was without sin took on our sins so that we would be pure, pure for the impure; righteous for the unrighteousness.

When God interrupts our plans, we should stop and pay attention to what is happening. Be the instrument God uses to show compassion to the one who needs it most.

	Pentecost 7 Year B Mark 6:1–13 Faith for Traveling Light for the Journey	
Watching *Mission Impossible* as a kid, I was always amazed how they accepted the assignment, got the job done.	Jesus and his disciples were going to Jesus's hometown where he grew up. He would know everyone and everyone would know him.	If refused to listen and rejected their teaching, to shake the dust from their feet and leave.
In previous scripture, Jesus healed the woman with hemorrhages and restored life to Jairus's daughter.	Most of his hometown folks were amazed at his teaching in the synagogue. After all, wasn't he the son of the carpenter and Mary?	Symbolic of Jews returning to Israel would shake the dust from their feet and leave.
These were first-time encounters yet they had great faith in Jesus and his ability to heal and restore.	Jesus was amazed at their unbelief and was not able to perform many miracles there.	The disciples' ministry was to proclaim the gospel, to heal, cast out demons, and to be with Jesus.
	Jesus commissions the disciples to go out in pairs and only take a staff and scandals.	God's mission comes with God's authority.
	Must learn to rely on God to provide all they need. Have faith that the community would believe their teachings and show them hospitality.	

Pentecost 7 Year B
Faith to Travel Light for the Journey
Mark 6:1–13

I remember watching *Mission Impossible* on television. I was amazed at the way they always completed their assignment. Normally there would be a scene where the main character was in a situation that you knew he would not escape this time. But somehow, he always came through.

In previous scripture, Jesus healed the woman with hemorrhage for twelve years and restored life to a twelve-year-old little girl. These were first-time encounters of Jesus. Both the woman and Jairus were commended by Jesus for their great faith. Jesus was able to do because the woman and Jairus both believed that he could. Now we get a glimpse of the other side of the coin.

Jesus and his disciples were going to Jesus's hometown where he grew up. He would know most of the people there, so he entered the synagogue on the Sabbath and began to teach. They were amazed at his teachings and began to question where his ability to do this came from. After all, wasn't he the son of the carpenter, the son of Mary? Even his brother James did not believe and become a follower of Christ. Most of the people were offended by Jesus. Jesus was not taken seriously in his own hometown. Jesus said, prophets are not without honor except in their hometown, and among their own kin and in their own house, words we still use today. Since he grew up with them and attended synagogue with them, he knew they were steeped in scripture and in prophecy. The people from his hometown were amazed at Jesus and he was amazed at their unbelief. Because of their unbelief, Jesus was not able to perform miracles there other than a few healings. Jesus left there and went to other villages and taught. Maybe this experience prompted Jesus of his next step in his ministry. He commissioned the disciples.

Jesus called his disciples together and sent them out in pairs and gave them the authority over the unclean spirits. His instructions to them were to take nothing but a staff and scandals. They were not to take bread, bag, money in their belts (no fanny packs,) and two tunics. Now this made for easier travels, yet it took faith to trust and rely on God to provide all they would need. God's provision would come through those who had faith and believed in their teachings. Hospitality has always been important to the Jews, and it still is. Jesus instructed them to enter a house and stay there until they left. He also told them if a house refused to welcome them and refused to listen to them and rejected them, they were to leave and shake the dust from their feet as a testimony against them. This strong symbolic action recalled the tradition that Jews returning to Israel would shake off the defiling dust of the Gentile lands from where they had traveled.[89] Their ministry was to proclaim the gospel, to heal, cast out demons, and to be with Jesus.[90]

When Jesus calls us to go, we must believe him and believe in him so that faith is the path we travel. I'm sure the disciples were overwhelmed with their assignment just as most of the time we are overwhelmed with ours. We wonder why God chose us, and we know that without God we could never accomplished any ministry. What we need to remember is that with God's mission comes God's authority to complete God's mission. It becomes mission possible. All you need is faith.

---

[89] *Feasting on the Word*, Year B. Volume 3 page 212

[90] Mark 3:13–19

	Pentecost 8 Year B Mark 6:14–29 But an Opportunity Came	
This passage of scripture is unique as Jesus is not the main character. We have Herod Antipas, son of Herod the Great, Herodias his wife, and John the Baptizer.	Baptized with water (Mark 1:8). Baptized with Holy Spirit (Mark 1:8).	Herod feared John and protected him. Was grieved he had to kill him but did it anyway (Mark 6:20, 26).
Yet if we read between the lines, Jesus is the main character. We will look at how John's life foreshadowed Jesus's life.	An opportunity came (Mark 6:21). Herod and Pilate became friends that day (Luke 23:12).	Pilate didn't want to kill Jesus, tried to get out of it, but he killed him anyway (Luke 23).
Birth announcement and name foretold (Luke 1:3–19, 30–31).	Not every time opportunity knocks should you open the door.	Beware of peer pressure and unhealthy advice.
Mistaken Identity: John 1:20–23 Mark 6:14–16	Herodias engineered John's death. Didn't have power to carry this out so relied on a governing official.	
Had disciples (Luke 6:29, Luke 6:12).	Religious leaders engineered Jesus's death. Didn't have power to carry this out, so they relied on a governing official to carry it out.	

Pentecost 8 Year B
But an Opportunity Came
Mark 6:14–29

This passage of scripture is unique as Jesus is not the main character. We have Herod Antipas, son of Herod the Great, Herodias his wife, his daughter, and John the Baptist. Yet if we read between the lines, Jesus is the main character. We will look at how John's life foreshadowed Jesus's life.

Gabriel announced the birth of John and foretold the name of the child.[91] Gabriel announced the birth of Jesus to Mary and told her what the child's name would be.[92] One announcement to a father and one to a mother.

Both John and Jesus were mistaken for other people. The religious leaders and people thought John the Baptist was either Elijah, a prophet, or the Christ.[93] These same people thought Jesus was Elijah, one of the prophets of old, or John the Baptist raised from the dead.[94] Notice how they mistook John for Christ and Christ for a resurrected John the Baptist.

John had disciples.[95] Jesus had disciples.[96]

Both baptized, John with water, and Jesus with the Holy Spirit.[97]

---

[91] Luke 1:3–19
[92] Luke 1:30–31
[93] John 1:20–23
[94] Mark 6:14–16
[95] Luke 6:29, Luke 6:12
[96] Mark 6:14–16
[97] Mark 1:8

The plot of John's death arose when an opportunity came.[98] Every opportunity that knocks on your door does not have to be opened. Look through the peephole and see who really is there and what they want. Jesus was doomed the day that Herod and Pilate became friends.[99] When there is a common cause, enemies become friends. They used one another. Be on guard not to fall for fake or false friendship.

Herodias engineered John's death. She had a grudge against him. She didn't have power to carry this out, so she relied on a governing official. Religious leaders engineered Jesus's death. They had a grudge against him but didn't have power to carry this out, so they relied on governing officials. We must beware of misusing our influence on those in office with power. We must check ourselves to see our true motives.

Herod feared John and protected him. Was grieved he had to kill him but did it anyway.[100] Pilate didn't want to kill Jesus, tried to get out of it, but he killed him anyway.[101] We must beware of peers pressuring us to do something that in our hearts we know we shouldn't do. We must have a strong sense of morals and values and stick with them. Look for opportunities not to get even but to do good. We must remember, "First, do no harm."[102]

---

[98] Mark 6:21
[99] Luke 23:12
[100] Mark 6:20, 26
[101] Luke 23
[102] John Wesley's Three Simple Rules

	Pentecost 9 Year B Mark 6:30–34, 53–56 When a Deserted Place Becomes Crowded	
A deserted place where there is no hustle or bustle, just peace and quiet.	Because Jesus's popularity was growing, all the people followed Jesus and the apostles and were there to greet them when they came ashore.	How do we react when our solitude is disrupted? For some is a relief as they find peace in a crowd.
Jesus had sent the apostles out on a mission to cast out demons, proclaim the gospel, and heal the sick.	When Jesus looked at the crowd, he had compassion for them. They were like sheep without a shepherd.	For some of us, it is in the quiet where we find peace and rest of our souls, bodies and minds before rejoining the crowd.
When the apostles reported back, Jesus told them to come away by themselves to a deserted place and rest.		Jesus often withdrew to a deserted place to be alone to pray (Luke 5:15–16, Luke 6:12, Matt. 14:23, Luke 22:39–41).
In Greek, the word rest means intermission from labor, refresh. What we use to call recess or playtime.		When our plans are disrupted, we need to withdraw from the crowd, get along with God, and pray.

Pentecost 9 Year B
When a Deserted Place Becomes Crowded
Mark 6:30–34, 53–56

A deserted place. No hustle or bustle, just peace and quiet. Don't we all, at times, dream of this. This is what Jesus desired for his apostles. He had sent the twelve out on a mission to cast out demons, proclaim the gospel, and heal the sick. They had reported back to Jesus all they had done. Jesus told them to come away by themselves to a deserted place and rest. He wanted them to come away by themselves, to leave all the things behind and have some down time and experience a respite from the mission. In this passage of scripture, the word rest means intermission from labor, refresh.[103] In grade school we would have called this recess or playtime.

Because Jesus's popularity was growing, all the people followed Jesus and the twelve on foot and were there to greet them when they came ashore. Jesus had compassion for them for they were like sheep without a shepherd and he began to teach them many things. Luke's gospel tells us that he taught them about the kingdom of God and healed those who needed to be cured.[104]

How do we react when our solitude is disrupted? For some of us it is a welcome relief from the quiet. Maybe some of us are more at peace in the middle of a crowd. For some of us, it is in the quiet where we find peace, a place to let our minds rest and energy be

---

[103] *Strong's Greek Dictionary* #373
[104] Luke 9:11

restored so that we will be able once morel to handle the crowds. Either way, Jesus is speaking to us today as he did then.

Jesus often went out to the mountain to be alone and pray. He would withdraw to deserted places and pray.[105] He prayed alone all night before selecting the twelve apostles.[106] After hearing of John the Baptist's death, Jesus withdrew from them in a boat to a deserted place to pray by himself privately.[107] Prior to his arrest and crucifixion, Jesus withdrew from his disciples about a stone's throw and prayed.[108]

So when our plans are disrupted, what should we do? We should withdraw, get alone with God, and pray.

---

[105] Luke 5:15–16
[106] Luke 6:12
[107] Luke 9:10–11
[108] Luke 22:39–41

Pentecost 10 Year B John 6:1–21 Miracle Times Three		
All four Gospels record the feeding of the five thousand. Hidden away in our scripture, we find two other miracles.	Realizing this, Jesus withdrew again to the mountain by himself.	When faced with what seems to be an impossible situation, how do we respond?
First miracle was five thousand fed from five barley loaves and two fish. Barley was the cheapest of the grains and was common bread for the poor.	The disciples while rowing to the other side, Jesus walks to them on the water. Jesus's power over nature displayed his deity.	Do we see obstacles or possibilities? Do we have a negative or positive attitude?
This miracle displayed Jesus's deity. Whatever we might need, Jesus's grace is sufficient.	Third miracle happened when the disciples wanted to take Jesus into the boat and immediately the boat reached where they were going.	Do we allow Jesus to walk to us or do we place obstacles in his way by trying to solve it ourselves?
Second miracle was Jesus walking on water. When the crowd saw what Jesus had done, they proclaimed him a prophet and wanted to make him king.	This miracle displayed Jesus's deity and power over time and space.	Do not be afraid but know Jesus is master over everything, and he is always on time.

Pentecost 10 Year B
Miracle Times Three
John 6:1–21

In all four Gospels—Matthew, Mark, Luke, and John—we find the feeding of the five thousand. Hidden away in our passage of John we find three other miracles. The first two are easy to find; they are very obvious. The third we might miss.

The first miracle is the feeding of the five thousand. Jesus asked where they could buy bread for all the people to eat. Philip only saw obstacles and replied, sixth months of wages would not be enough to buy even a little bread for all the people. But Andrew saw possibilities and told Jesus he had seen a boy with five barley loaves and two fish. Jesus tells him to get them. Barley was the cheapest of the grains and was common bread among the poor. Then Jesus broke the bread then blessed it. The disciples handed out pieces of bread and fish and had twelve baskets of bread leftover. Scripture tells us there were five thousand men, but we have no number of women and children. Still it was a miracle that so many people could eat and be satisfied from only five barely loaves and two fish. This miracle displayed the deity of Jesus in that whatever our need might be. Jesus's grace is more than sufficient.

The next miracle we find Jesus walking on water. When the crowd saw what Jesus had done, they proclaimed him a prophet and wanted to make him king. Realizing this, Jesus withdrew again to the mountain by himself. Notice the word *again*. Many times, Jesus withdrew to the mountain to be by himself. The disciples got in a boat to travel back to the other side. A storm arose and the disciples saw Jesus walking on the water toward the boat. This miracle showed the deity of Jesus as he had power over the water. We can know that when a storm appears in our lives, Jesus will walk to us regardless of where we are. We have no need to fear.

The third miracle is at the end of our scripture passage. When Jesus walked on water to get to the disciples' boat, they wanted to take him into the boat with them and immediately the boat reached the land toward where they were going. Jesus showed his deity by demonstrating his power over time and space. The disciples had been rowing for three or four miles, but with Jesus in the boat, in a flash, they reached their destination.

When faced with what seems to be an impossible situation, how do we respond? Do we see obstacles or possibilities? In other words, do we have a negative attitude or a positive one? Do we have enough faith to believe in the possibilities? Do we allow Jesus to walk to us or do we place obstacles in his way by trying to solve it ourselves? We must remember that Jesus is sufficient regardless of what is needed. Do not be afraid but know Jesus is master over everything.

	Pentecost 11 Year B John 6:24–35 Soul Food	
Previously the feeding of the five thousand and Jesus walked on water.	Jesus told them not to work for food that perishes but for the food that endures for eternal life.	Crowd wanted to see a sign to show they should believe in Jesus. They had just received a sign, a miracle, when Jesus fed them with barley loaves and two fish.
Crowd looked for Jesus. Asked him when he got there.	Food provided during the Exodus was perishable. The food that endures for eternal life comes through Jesus.	They asked for the bread always. They asked for the right thing but with the wrong reason. They never wanted to be physically hungry again.
Jesus revealed the real motive of the crowd. They were not looking for signs; they were looking for him to give them food to eat. Rice Christians.	Eternal life does not speak of a future life in heaven but is a metaphor for living *now* in the unending presence of God.	What about us? Are we part of the crowd? Are we looking for Jesus for the wrong reason? Do we ask for signs to prove he is who he says he is?
The crowd wore blinders and could not see beyond the actual feeding for the miracle it was and for what it revealed.	The crowd asked what they must do to perform the works of God. Crowd understood work as a performance of a certain act.	Each one of us has a hole in their soul, looking to fill it with something. We need to fill it with Jesus.
	Jesus meant work as faith in God.	

Pentecost 11 Year B
Soul Food
John 6:24–35

On television they will show a recap of the previous show before they start the next episode. Well, previously on the Jesus channel, we watched as five thousand people were fed with five loaves of barley and two fish with plenty left over. Then we saw Jesus walk on water. Now we pick up with the crowd looking for Jesus, getting into boats trying to find him. Once they found him, they inquired how he got there. They hadn't witnessed the miracle of the boat reaching the other side immediately. Jesus responded, "Very truly I tell you, you are looking for me, not because you saw signs, but because you ate your fill of the loaves." In nineteenth century China, many came to the churches because they were given food to eat. They were hungry and the church provided a need. When they no longer received food, they no longer attended church, thus the name "Rice Christian."[109]

This crowd wore blinders and could not see beyond their physical need being met to the presence of God in Jesus. They had an encounter with God but did not recognize him. The feeding of the five thousand should have been a sign to them that Jesus was from God and had been sent from God. But all they were focused on was being fed the bread and fish.

Jesus continued, "Do not work for food that perishes, but for the food that endures for eternal life, which the Son of Man will give you. For it is on him that God the Father has set his seal." The food

---

[109] *Feasting on the Word* Year B, volume 3, p 308

provided during the Exodus was perishable. The food that endures for eternal life comes only from the Son of Man. Eternal life does not speak of immediately or a future life in heaven, but is a metaphor for living *now* in the unending presence of God.

The crowd then asked what they must do to perform the works of God. The crowd understood work as a performance of a certain act, but for Jesus, work is faith in God. The crowd wanted to see a sign to show them they should believe in Jesus and cited an example of Moses giving them manna in the wilderness. Jesus explained that Moses did not give them the manna but it was from God. The Father gives true bread from heaven himself.

The crowd didn't get it. They asked Jesus to give them this bread always. They didn't understand what Jesus was trying to tell them. They were asking for the right thing for the wrong reasons. They wanted to never be hungry again and wanted food to eat. They didn't get it that Jesus was the bread of heaven who came to earth. They missed it.

What about us? Why do we go looking for Jesus? Is it to ask him for what we think is best for us or that which will fill our hungry hearts? Do we ask for signs so that we can be sure Jesus is who he says he is?

Each one of us has a hole in their soul and is looking for something to fill it. Most often we will it with things. We are looking for soul food instead of food for the soul. Do we go looking for Jesus just to be in the presence of God; to just sit and be still in the silence with God and wait for him to speak to us, to fill ourselves to overflowing with his presence? Most of us don't. We go with our grocery list of items we want or outcomes of certain situations that affect us. Jesus desires us to seek him this day so that we may have life and have it more abundantly. If we feel we have been given the short straw in the draw of life, we need to go look for Jesus, seek him out right now. Sit with him. Let him be the one to fill us to overflowing with what satisfies the soul, the heart, the mind, our total being. Him.

Pentecost 12 Year B
John 6:35, 41–51
Come to Jesus

The crowd didn't get it. Now we will look at the religious leaders and how they responded to Jesus.

Jesus states no one can come to him unless drawn by the father who sent him. Through prevenient grace, God woos us.

Jesus explains the manna and the living bread. Manna met a temporary physical need. Jesus is a permanent solution to a spiritual need, and we have eternal life.

Jesus makes another I AM statement. "I Am the bread of life. Anyone who comes to me will never hunger or thirst again."

At this point we are at a crossroads with free will to choose. What path will we follow?

I AM the living bread. Anyone who eats will live forever. The bread is my flesh that I will give for the life of the world.

Jesus is speaking about a spiritual need, not a physical one.

Will we be obedient to God? Obedient only when convenient for us? Continue on our selfish path or turn our backs to God?

"For God so loved the world that he gave his only begotten son that whosoever believes in him shall not perish but have everlasting life."

The Jews, the religious leaders of the council, complained about Jesus. They didn't get it either.

Obeying God is a decision we make first with our minds. Then our obedience moves from our head to our heart and then to deep down in our souls.

The religious leaders knew the parents of Jesus, so it did not make sense to them that he would say he came from heaven.

Pentecost 1 Year B
Come to Jesus
John 6:35, 41–51

Previously we saw how the crowd "missed it," how they asked for a miracle, a sign when they had just experienced one. Now we join the religious leaders to see their response to Jesus.

Jesus made another I Am statement: I am the bread of life and those who come to me will never be hungry or thirsty. Jesus is talking about a spiritual need, not a physical one. The Jews, the religious leaders of the council, complained about Jesus. They didn't get it. They didn't understand. They knew the parents of Jesus and there was nothing supernatural about them. They believed nothing could come from heaven that wasn't supernatural. So it didn't add up.

Jesus told them not to complain among themselves for no one can come to Jesus unless drawn by the Father who sent him. Through prevenient grace God woos us. At this point, we are at a crossroads and have free will to decide which path we will take. Will we put our will aside and be obedient to Jesus and do God's will? Will we decide to only follow Jesus when it is convenient for us? Will we continue our journey of selfishness? Or completely turn our backs to God?

It is up to us. Obeying God's will is a decision we have to first make with our mind. As we continue on our faith walk, our belief will move from our mind into our heart and then move to deep down in our soul. Through the Holy Spirit, we are taught by God about Jesus. The deeper our understanding, the deeper our commitment and in the present we experience God's presence through our relationship with Jesus.

Jesus tried to explain to the Jews the difference between the manna and him, the living bread. Both did come from God, but the manna met a physical need and was a temporary fix. The manna sustained them for a day but they were back for more the next day. The manna did not sustain their lives for they all eventually died. Jesus was a permanent solution to a spiritual need. Through belief in Jesus, we are granted eternal life, life everlasting. And we can have that type of life now.

Jesus continued, "I Am the living bread. Anyone who eats of this bread will live forever. And the bread I will give for the life of the world is my flesh."

"For God so loved the world that he gave his only begotten Son, so that whoever believes in him will not perish but have everlasting life."[110]

Have we already come to Jesus or are we still engaged in the battle of the wills? There is so much freedom to be found in letting go and doing God's will. We know God's will is the best thing for us, and we also know there will be a little pain and suffering that goes along with it. But remember that is momentary. For "We do not lose heart.... For this slight momentary affliction is preparing us for an eternal weight of glory beyond all measure, because we look not at what can be seen but at what cannot be seen; for what can be seen is temporary but what cannot be seen is eternal."[111]

---

[110] John 3:16
[111] 2 Corinthians 4:16–18

	Pentecost 13 Year B John 6:51–58 Consuming Jesus	
Throughout the sixth chapter of John, Jesus relates everlasting life and eternal life to believing.	Jesus compares manna to the living bread from heaven.	Something mystical happens when we partake of communion.
It would benefit us to remember this as it will help us with our understanding of eating his flesh and drinking of his blood.	Manna was a temporary solution to a physical need, which did not have an everlasting effect.	When we celebrate the Eucharist, the Last Supper, we abide with Jesus, the living bread.
When we hear these words we think of the last supper and our own communion with the Trinity.	A lot of us are looking for a temporary fix. Looking for instant gratification, not the long-term obligation to a program.	When we partake of Communion, we are saying that we believe. What do we believe? All found in the Apostle's Creed.

Pentecost 13 Year B
Consuming Jesus
John 6:51–58

All through the sixth chapter of John, Jesus relates everlasting life, eternal life to believing. We wonder how many more times he needs to repeat it. In today's scripture, it is to our benefit to remember all the times he has taught this as it will help us with our understanding of eating of his flesh and drinking of his blood.

Of course, when we hear those words we think of the last supper and our own communion with the Trinity. John uses metaphors throughout his gospel. A metaphor is a word used symbolically of another. We also call these analogies. Jesus was not speaking literally of his flesh and blood but what they symbolized, his death. The Jewish religious leaders took it literally and they were once again complaining among themselves.

Jesus compares the manna to the living bread from heaven. The manna was a temporary solution to a physical need, which did not have everlasting effect. Each day the Israelites had to gather the manna for that day's nourishment. Compared to the living bread, Jesus's flesh and blood, manna was temporary. Most people are looking for the temporary fix: the quick way to lose a few pounds, or quit smoking, or kick an addiction problem. They are looking for instant gratification, not the long-term obligation to the program, which takes time.

When we partake of Communion, something mystical happens. We are joined with the great cloud of witnesses and the trinity as we remember the sacrifice Jesus made for us.

When we celebrate the Eucharist, the Last Supper, we are abiding with Jesus, the living bread. We ingest him and he is in us. Those who abide with Jesus will have eternal fulfillment, not temporary nourishment. Jesus gives us life everlasting, eternal life. Jesus lives because of the Father and we live because of Jesus.

When we partake of Communion, we are saying that we believe. What do we believe? It's all in the Apostle's Creed.

> I believe in God, the Father Almighty, maker of heaven
> and earth;
> And in Jesus Christ his only Son, our Lord;
> who was conceived by the Holy Spirit,
> born of the Virgin Mary,
> suffered under Pontus Pilate,
> was crucified, dead, and buried;*
> the third day he rose from the dead;
> he ascended into heaven,
> and sitteth at the right hand of God the Father Almighty;
> from thence he shall come to judge the quick and the dead.
> I believe in the Holy Spirit,
> the holy catholic[112] church,
> the communion of saints,
> the forgiveness of sins,
> the resurrection of the body,
> and the life everlasting. Amen.

When we take Communion we invite all to the table. The only requirement is that they believe.

---

[112] church universal

	Pentecost 14 Year B John 6:56–59 Accepting Difficult Teaching	
Jesus taught the disciples to abide in him they must eat of his flesh and drink of his blood. Disciples ask who would be able to accept such difficult teaching.	Reasons we find the passage difficult to accept.	Results of not accepting difficult teaching.
Ever read a passage and declare it too difficult to accept? Turn the other cheek, love your neighbor; if you don't love your brother you can't love God.	We don't understand. Read what comes before and after to get it in context. History in OT requires research. Check cross-references.	Some will leave the faith and search for a more comfortable venue, scripture which tickles the ears (2 Tim. 4:4).
	Scripture reveals a character flaw in us. It steps on our toes.	Some will grumble and complain to anyone who will listen (James 4:1).
	Crowds followed Jesus because of the signs and healings he did. When the tough got going, the weak fell away. Jesus asks the twelve, "Do you also want to leave?"	Some will take the lesson to heart and change their behavior, which changes their character (Rom. 5:1–5).
		Only through accepting difficult teaching and putting it into practice are we able to undergo true growth and change and spiritual transformation.

Pentecost 14 Year B
Accepting Difficult Teaching
John 6:56–59

Previously Jesus taught the disciples that in order to abide in him they must eat of his flesh and drink of his blood. Now the disciples questioned who would be able to accept such difficult teaching.

Have we ever read a passage in the Bible and declared it too difficult to accept? Maybe we have read where we are to love our neighbor or turn the other cheek.[113] It might be God is love, and if you do not love your brother, you can't love God.[114] There are many more but let's look at some of the reasons we might find this difficult to accept.

We might not understand the passage. We must read what comes before and after to place a passage of scripture into perspective. Many times, a passage in the New Testament has a history in the Old Testament, and a little research is necessary. There are times we will have to read and reread the scripture and check cross-references.

Another reason for finding scripture difficult is it reveals something in us, a character flaw that we would rather not address. Or possibly the passage instructs us to do something we do not want to do. You might say both of these reasons can be summed up as it steps on our toes.

We have seen Jesus perform many miracles and signs and the countless healings. The crowds were following him because of these

---

[113] Matthew 22:39, Matthew 5:39
[114] 1 John 4:21

153

signs and healings. But when the tough got going, the weak fell away. When the disciples started leaving Jesus, he asked the twelve if they also wished to go away. Can't we just hear the hurt in this question?

Because we refused to accept scripture as truth, there are several results we will face. Think of ourselves at a crossroad. What we do next reveals how we accept difficult teaching. Some will leave the faith and search for a more comfortable venue, scripture which tickles the ears.[115] Some will grumble and complain to anyone who will listen,[116] while others will take the lesson to heart and change their behavior, which changes their character.

> Therefore, since we are justified by faith, we have peace with God through our Lord Jesus Christ, through whom we have obtained access to this grace in which we stand; and we boast in our hope of sharing the glory of God. And not only that, but we also boast in our sufferings, knowing that suffering produces endurance, and endurance produces character, and character produces hope, and hope does not disappoint us, because God's love has been poured into our hearts through the Holy Spirit that has been given to us.[117]

Only through accepting difficult teaching and putting it to practice are we able to undergo true growth and change and true spiritual transformation.

---

[115] 2 Timothy 4:4
[116] James 4:1
[117] Romans 5:1–5

	Pentecost 15 Year B Mark 7:1–8, 14–15, 21–23 Give a Hoot, Don't Pollute	
Today's scripture is a contrast in outward appearances of religious leaders and the heart of a follower of Christ.	Jesus was questioned why he did not make his disciples follow the tradition of the elders.	What about us? Do we fail to understand? Or do we give a hoot and not pollute our hearts?
The Pharisees and scribes were all about appearance and how they were perceived by the community.	Tradition of the elders was a series of man-made rules to enhance the ceremonial laws of the Jews. They were not based on scripture.	In order to safeguard our hearts, we need to ask God to test it (Ps. 26:2–3).
Made a show out of washing their hands, foods bought at market, and their plates and cups.	Jesus rebuked the Pharisees and scribes with Old Testament scripture (Isa. 29:13).	Ask God to cleanse our hearts (Ps. 51:10).
The Pharisees held Jesus accountable for the disciples' unwashed hands they used to eat.	Jesus called them hypocrites, actors with masks playing a part, and accused them of putting appearance of piety before true obedience.	Ask God to help us keep our hearts with all vigilance (Prov. 4:23).
	Jesus instructed the crowd to listen and understand. The disciples questioned him in private. Jesus responded, "Then do you also fail to understand?"	Ask God to guard our hearts with his peace (Phil. 4:5–7).

Pentecost 15 Year B
Give a Hoot and Don't Pollute Your Heart
Mark 7:1–8, 14–15, 21–23

In today's scripture reading we find a contrast between outside appearance of the religious leaders and the hearts of a disciple of Christ. Today, if we follow Jesus, we also are his disciples.

The Pharisees and scribes, who were the religious leaders, we're more concerned about outward appearance and how they were perceived by the community rather than true obedience. They made a show of everything including washing their hands, food, and dishes.

When the Pharisees and scribes from Jerusalem observed the disciples of Jesus eating with unclean hands, they held Jesus accountable for his disciples' actions and accused them of not following the tradition of the elders. The tradition of the elders was a series of rules meant to enhance the ceremonial laws of the Jews. Its authority was not supported by Scripture.[118]

Jesus called the Pharisees and scribes hypocrites. Hypocrites originally referred to actors wearing a mask and playing a part.[119] Jesus accuses them of putting the appearance of piety before true obedience. He responded with Old Testament Scripture, Isaiah prophesies rightly about hypocrites, as it is written, "These people honors me with their lips, but their hearts are far from me; in vain

---

[118] New King James Study Bible
[119] New King James Study Bible

do they worship me, teaching human precepts as doctrine."[120] Jesus continues, "You abandon the commandment of God and hold to human tradition."

Then Jesus called the crowd and said to them, "Listen to me, all of you, and understand: there is nothing outside of a person that by going in can defile, but the things that come out are what defiles." In private, the disciples asked Jesus about the parable. Jesus responded with a question, "Then do you also fail to understand?" Jesus explained whatever goes into a person cannot defile since it enters not the heart but the stomach for it is from within the human heart that evil intentions come. John Wesley wrote, "Pollution arises from the heart."[121]

Today we are not above the evil intentions of the heart. Like the Pharisees and scribes, we are clothed in righteousness as we wound some and ignore others. Laws are needed to organize community. Doctrine is needed to articulate our beliefs. However, when we began to worship or bow down to what gives us a sense of order, we no longer are faithful to God. The breach between true spirituality and man-made traditions widen. How do we misinterpret what is important to God? We missed the big picture.

Cory Booker, the first African-American junior senator from New Jersey, said the following:

> Before you speak to me about your religion, first show it to me in how you treat other people; before you tell me how much you love God, show me in how much you love all his children; before you preach to me of your passion for your faith, teach me about it through your compassion for your neighbors. In the end, I'm not interested in what you have to tell or sell as I am in how you choose to live and give.

---

[120] Isaiah 29:13
[121] Wesley Study Bible

What about us? Do we fail to understand, or do we give a hoot and don't pollute our hearts? What about our hearts? Are we worshipping God but in our hearts we have return to Egypt?[122]

We must ask God to cleanse our hearts.[123]

We must ask God to test our hearts and minds.[124]

We must ask God to keep our hearts with all vigilance. And we must allow God's peace to guard our hearts.

[122] Exodus 7:39

[123] Psalms 51:10

[124] Psalms 26:2–3

	Pentecost 16 Year B Mark 7:24–37 What about Us?	
Tyre was located on the Mediterranean coast, northwest Galilee in a predominantly Gentile area.	Next Jesus travels to Decapolis. People brought a deaf man with a speech impediment to be healed.	Both encounters, the affected were not the ones who asked for healing. It was other people. What about us?
The woman is described as a gentile, and when she heard of Jesus she went to him and asked him to rid her daughter of an unclean spirit.	Jesus took him from the crowd and placed his fingers in the man's ears, then spat and touched his tongue. The man was healed.	Both encounters were with Gentiles. It's possible that Jesus accepting the woman opened the doors for Gentiles. What about us?
Previously we saw Jesus telling the Pharisees and scribes defilement of a person comes from within. The girl would have been thought of as defiled.	The man represented the people including Jesus's disciples' inability to hear, listen, and understand.	Both encounters resulted in Jesus not only healing but restoring the person to community. What about us?
We are shocked at Jesus's reply, but the Gentile woman stood her ground and responded correctly.		May those who have ears listen and understand the teaching of the Lord.
Jesus proclaimed his ministry was for Jews. His acceptance of the woman based on her faith, opened the door for Jesus's ministry to Gentiles.		

Pentecost 16 Year B
What about Us?
Mark 7:24–37

<hr>

Tyre was located on the Mediterranean coast northwest of Galilee in a predominantly Gentile area. The woman is described as a Gentile of Syrophoenician origin. Immediately she heard about Jesus and went to him and bowed down at his feet. This demonstrated her submissiveness to Jesus. She begged Jesus to heal her daughter of an unclean spirit. Previously we saw Jesus's confrontation with the Pharisees and scribes about what defiles. This woman's daughter was defiled with an unclean spirit.

Then Jesus told her, "Let the children be fed first; for it is not fair to take the children's food and throw it to the dogs." Although it is unclear if little children refers to Israel as a whole or just the disciples, but the meaning of his statement was very clear.

The woman spoke back to Jesus saying even dogs under the table ate the children's crumbs. She was saying I know I'm a Gentile and I am beneath you but will settle for any crumb you will give me. Underneath this conversation is Jesus proclaiming his ministry for Israel, not the Gentiles. His acceptance of the woman was based on her faith and opened the doorway for Jesus's ministry to extend to the Gentiles.

Next Jesus traveled to the area known as the Decapolis (ten little cities) or a league of cities. Decapolis was primarily a Gentile community. Some people brought a man to Jesus to be healed. He had a speech impediment and was also deaf. Jesus took the man away from the crowd and he was healed immediately.

The man represented people, including Jesus's disciples, concerning their inability to hear clearly and grasp the meaning of Jesus's teaching. So many of us today still fail to hear, listen, and understand.

In both encounters the afflicted were not the ones who asked for healing. It was a mother and friends. What about us? As followers of Christ, we are called to step out in faith and asked Jesus to heal. Our faith can make others well. Do we pray for others? Do we kneel at the throne and intercede on behalf of others?

In both encounters they were Gentiles. It's possible that Jesus's acceptance of the Syrophoenician woman opened the door for the deaf man to receive healing. Jesus looked beyond his infirmity and the woman's status and saw them as children of God. What about us? Do we look at others and always see the differences, or do we see a beloved child of God? Are there people we have deemed unworthy of our time and our faith? Do we determine a person's worth based on their status? Do we accept diversity?

Lastly, these two encounters with Jesus not only healed but also restored them to community. No longer was the little girl thought of as evil or the man as sinful. What about us? Are we accepting of those who have less than us, or believe differently from us, who wish to be in community with us? In our hearts do we see them as "those people"?

May those who have ears listen and understand the teaching of the Lord.

Pentecost 17 Year B Mark 8:27–38 Carry Your Own Cross		
Jesus and his disciples traveled to Caesarea Philippi, which was predominantly Gentile territory, and Jesus asked them two questions.	Jesus taught them about his impending suffering, rejection by religious leaders, his death, and his resurrection.	In Jesus's time the cross was a symbol of death.
Who do people say I am? The disciples responded John the Baptist, Elijah, and one of the prophets.	Peter rebuked Jesus. He had answered the question correctly but didn't understand the meaning of Messiah.	As followers of Christ, each one of us must also carry the symbol of death. Our death is death of self, denying ourselves.
Second question: Who do you say I am? Peter responded, "The Messiah."	Jesus rebuked Peter saying he was setting his mind not on divine things but on human things.	We must give up our will for the will of God.
	Jesus told the crowd, "If any want to become my followers, let them deny themselves and take up their cross and follow me."	Each person's call will be different; therefore, each cross, each sacrifice will be different.
	Once we understand who Jesus is, we must answer the call to discipleship.	In our death of self we find eternal life. For those who want to save their life will lose it, and those who lose their life for Jesus and the gospel will save it.

Pentecost 17 Year B
Who Do You Say I Am?
Mark 8:27–38

Jesus and his disciples went to Caesarea Philippi, which was predominantly Gentile territory. On the way Jesus asked his disciples two questions. "Who do people say I am?" The disciples responded, John the Baptist, Elijah, and one of the prophets. The second question was, "Who do you say I am?" This time only Peter answered. He proclaimed Jesus as Messiah. Peter got the correct response but didn't understand what it meant to be the Messiah. If Peter had understood, he would not have reacted the way he did when Jesus spoke of his suffering, death, and resurrection. Peter did not want Jesus to suffer, which is understandable. Jesus rebuked Peter and told him he was only looking at earthly things, not things that are eternal. Jesus addressed the crowd and says, "If any of you want to become one of my followers, let them deny themselves and take up their cross and follow me."

What should we learn about today's scripture?

These days, when people are asked who is Jesus, a variety of answers will surface based on a person's age.[125] The older generation will say Jesus is the Son of God and he was conceived by the Holy Spirit and Mary was his mother. This age group will more likely believe in the tenet of their churches. They will also have a strong sense of community and believe that it is important to attend worship and other social event with the church.

---

[125] The Barna Research Group

Some of the younger generation believe Jesus was a nice man, a good man. They do not consider his divinity at all. Some believe that he was a spiritual leader or teacher just like Mohammed or Buddha. Others say they believe there is a God, but they do not follow his commandments. And then others say there is no God.

Who do we say Jesus is? We know the correct answer, what is expected of us to say, but what do we really believe. An old country song sums it up, "You've got to stand for something, or you'll fall for anything." We must know Jesus in our heart and his teachings down in our soul. This foundational belief will keep us from believing what others might say. We must prepare ourselves to give an answer for the reason for our hope. What we believe is found in the Apostle's Creed.

As a follower of Christ, we must answer the call to discipleship. In Jesus's time the cross was a symbol of death. Each one of his followers must also carry the symbol of death with us. Our death is the death of self, denying ourselves. We must give up our will for God's will. Each person's call is different; therefore each cross and each sacrifice will be different. In our death of self, we find eternal life. "For those who want to save their life will lose it, and those who lose their life for my sake, and for the sake of the gospel will save it."

	Pentecost 18 Year B Mark 9:30–37	
Jesus and his disciples traveled secretly through Galilee. On the way, Jesus taught them again about his death and resurrection.	First will be last. Opposite of what society believes. All through life we are taught to be first to be better than the next and that our worth is based on wealth.	The disciples had wrong priorities. What about us? What consumes us? If God is not at the top of the list, reorganization is needed.
Once again the disciples did not understand what Jesus was saying but were too afraid to ask.	To be a disciple of Christ, we must be last and servant of all. The twelve did not understand the teaching of the cross.	The teaching of the cross is love for others and sacrifice for others. We must be willing to die to self, put our wants and needs last, beneath the needs of others.
When they reached Capernaum, Jesus asked the twelve what they were arguing about on the way. They were silent.	During these times, a person's fame and wealth was based on the company they kept.	We should not think too highly of ourselves. The more we think of ourselves, the less anyone else will think.
Disciples had argued who was the greatest. Jesus saw another teaching opportunity.	Jesus welcomed the powerless, and in so doing they became the powerful.	Live in harmony with one another; do not be haughty, but associate with the lowly, do not claim to be wiser than you are (Rom. 12:16).
Whoever wants to be first must be last of all. Whoever welcomes one such child in my name welcomes me and the one who sent me.		We must put away pride and ambition and focus on people. We are here to serve. Power is found when serving others.

Pentecost 18 Year B
Power to Serve
Mark 9:30–37

Jesus, not wanting people to know, traveled secretly through Galilee with the disciples. He was teaching them once again about his death and resurrection. Once again, the disciples did not understand. Once they reached Capernaum, Jesus asked them what they had argued about on the way there. The disciples were silent. Can we just imagine the deafening sound of silence while Jesus waited for an answer? Just picture the disciples shuffling their feet as they stared at the ground trying to avoid Jesus's face. Jesus knew what they had discussed and he broke the silence, saying, "Whoever wants to be first must be last of all and servant of all." Jesus saw another teaching opportunity and took a little child and said, "Whoever welcomes one of these in my name, welcomes me and the one who sent me." What were the lessons Jesus was trying to teach?

First must be last and servant of all. This is the total opposite of what society teaches us. All through life we are taught to be first, to be better than the next or better than the one and our worth is based on wealth. But to be a disciple of Christ, we must be last and servant of all. The disciples did not understand the teaching of the cross. Sacrifice. You die to self and live for others. It is putting our wants and needs beneath the needs of others.

Whoever welcomes a child in my name also welcomes me and the one who sent me. During these times, a person's fame and wealth were based on the company they kept. Children were not very high on the social status ladder. Jesus welcomed the powerless, and in so doing they became powerful.

We should not think too highly of ourselves. The more we think of ourselves, the less anyone else will think of us.

> Live in harmony with one another; do not be haughty, but associate with the lowly, do not claim to be wiser than you are.[126]
>
> As for those who in the present age are rich, command them not to be haughty, or to set their hopes on the uncertainty of riches, but rather on God who richly provides us with everything for our enjoyment. They are to do good, to be rich in good works, generous, and ready to share, thus storing up for themselves the treasure of a good foundation for the future, so that they may take hold of the life that really is life.[127]

We must put away pride and ambition and focus on people. We are to serve. Power is found when serving others.

---

[126] Romans 12:16
[127] 1 Timothy 6:17

	Pentecost 19 Year B Mark 9:38–50 Pass the Salt Please	
We are called to be in community. In community we have a place where we are known and recognized and are given a sense of self.	Stay in community without being exclusive.	When we exude others, we are doing harm as nothing about exclusiveness is good. We can't stay in love with God if we do not love others.
Community helps form and shape our beliefs and our morals.	Be open and welcoming, fully accepting while supporting all other persons, enabling them to fully participate in the life of the Church, community, and world.	The many purposes of salt: clears, cleans, deodorizes, restore, relieves, conditions, keeps, exfoliate.
Danger of community being so focused on itself that those outside the circle are overlooked.	Being inclusive without losing our salt.	The tree of our core values. Roots—God the Father, Jesus Christ the Son, and the Holy Spirit.
	Three simple rules: do no harm, do good, and stay in love with God.	Trunk—Christ has died, Christ has risen, Christ will come again.
		Branches things we do which produce fruit.

Pentecost 19 Year B
Pass the Salt Please
Mark 9:38–50

We are called to be in community. It is in community we have a place we are known and recognized. It gives us a sense of self, of identity. Community helps form and shape our beliefs and our morals. But a community may be so focused on itself that those outside the circle are overlooked. So how do we stay in community without being exclusive? How do we become inclusive without losing our saltiness?[128]

In the 2012 *Book of Discipline* of the United Methodist Church, inclusiveness means, "Openness, acceptance, and support that enables all persons to participate in the life of the church, the community and the world; therefore, inclusiveness denies every semblance of discrimination. The services of worship of every local church of the United Methodist church shall be open to all persons. The mark of an inclusive society is one in which all persons are open, welcoming, fully accepting and supporting of all other persons, enabling them to participate fully in the life of the church, the community and the world. A further mark of inclusiveness is the setting of church activities in facilities accessible to persons with disabilities."[129]

How can we be inclusive without losing our saltiness, our core values?

---

[128] *Feasting on the Word* Year B. Vol. 4
[129] 2012 *Book of Discipline* of the United Methodist Church, Section VI

In the book, *Three Simple Rules*, Reuben Job sums it all up with "do no harm, do good, stay in love with God." When we exclude others for whatever reason, we are not honoring that person or giving their life worth. We are harming them on a personal level. We are called to love one another just as Christ loves us. Most importantly, when we are exclusive, we are not following the teachings of Jesus. The Jewish faith has a strong sense of community. Jesus didn't exclude anyone except maybe the Pharisees, scribes, and leaders who were highly exclusive.

We are to do good. There is nothing good about exclusiveness. Leaving others out intentionally is not of God, and we know God is good. We are to stay in love with God. We must have daily communication with God through prayer and reading the Word. When others are included into our group, we learn from them and they learn from us. But we must have a strong foundation in our core values and not lose our saltiness.

Salt has many purposes; some you may be familiar with such as seasoning food and easing a sore throat. It also clears flower residue in a vase, removes wine from carpet, removes watermark from wood table, keeps window and windshield frost free, restores a sponge, relives a bee sting, deodorize sneakers, conditions hard water, prevents towels from fading, and exfoliates skin.

Think of a tree and its roots and branches. In our lives the roots of our core value is found in Father God, Jesus Christ his Son, and the Holy Spirit. The trunk of our value is Christ has died, Christ has risen, and Christ will come again. The many branches are the things we do that produce fruit such as communion, worship, Bible study, helping others, and many more. It is our action that produces fruit and helps us stay in love with God.

We must keep our root system and the trunk of our tree intact, but there are many ways we stay in love with God. We should be accepting of all and encourage them to go and produce fruit.

	Pentecost 20 Year B Mark 10:1–16 Me? Adultery?	
Pharisees question Jesus about divorce. Satan and the Pharisees seem to be the only ones who test Jesus.	Under Torah, only men could receive a divorce and only a woman is accused of adultery.	What about our relationship with God? Have we committed adultery against him? Exodus 20: place no god above me.
God's intentions were for a man and a woman to be joined and the two will become one flesh.	Jesus's culture marriage was not romantic love but the transfer of a woman from her father's to her husband's home.	Our mistresses? Food, sports teams, compulsive buying, friends.
Moses issued the divorce certificate because of the hardness of the Israelites' hearts.	She had no protection, so Moses issued a divorce certificate so she could enter another man's home without committing adultery.	Our relationship with God should be like a marriage. God pursued us, wooed us, and we said yes to an eternal relationship.
	Isaiah 54:5 Ephesians 5:25	Nothing can separate us from the love of God. We have freedom of choice. Choose wisely as who or what will have first place in your heart, in your life.

Pentecost 20 Year B
Me? Adultery?
Mark 10:2–26

In the scripture reading today we find the Pharisees questioning Jesus about divorce. Have you ever noticed Satan and the Pharisees are the only ones to test Jesus? We learn that God's intentions were for a man and a woman to be joined and the two would become one flesh. It was Moses who issued the divorce certificate because of the hardness of the Israelites' hearts.

Under Torah, Jewish law, not Roman law, only men could receive a divorce. The woman was prohibited from petitioning for divorce. Under these same laws, only a woman could be accused of adultery. During these times, marriage in Jesus's culture was not for a romantic love but rather the passing of a woman from her father's house to the house of her husband. She had no rights, so the law did not protect her. Do you see the inequality here? Do you see any semblance of justice?

Jesus explains God meant for marriage to be permanent, but man had made it something else. On a whim, a man could kick his wife out of his home, leaving her with no support, and there was nothing she could do about it. She had no recourse. Moses issued a certificate of divorce so that the woman could enter another man's home so she would be provided for.

Adultery entered the picture when a married woman had relations with a man who was not her husband. But Jesus expands that definition to include a man's infidelity toward his own wife. Isaiah 54:5 tells us that we are to love our Maker who is our husband.

Ephesians 5:25 says, husbands are to love their wives as Jesus loves the church, and this was not happening. Jesus sacrificed who he was and what he had so we would be able to have this marriage relationship with God.

But what about our relationship with God? Have we committed adultery against him? The greatest commandment is Hear, O Israel: The Lord our God, the Lord is one. Love the Lord your God with all your heart and with all your soul and with all your mind and with all your strength.[130] One of the Ten Commandments is you will place no gods before the Lord our God.[131] If we stop and really think about this and pray about this, we will see we all have many mistresses. Do we love food more than we do God? Do we place our favorite sports team above worshipping God? What about shopping? Are we compulsive buyers, buyers of things not needed? What about our friends? Do we choose the crowd over God? And the list goes on and on. You see, adultery occurs when we place things and people above God.

We should think of our relationship with God as a marriage. We divorce ourselves from God when we hardened our hearts toward him and his commands. God doesn't change his love for us. If we no longer feel as close to God, we are the ones who moved. God pursued us, wooed us, and we said yes and we were joined together from that day forward. There is nothing we can do that will separate us from God's love.[132] Even when we move, God still loves us. We have the freedom to choose what takes the number one priority in our hearts and our lives. Choose wisely.

---

[130] Mark 12:29–30
[131] Exodus 20
[132] Romans 8:31–39

	Pentecost 21 Year B Mark 10:17–31 What's in It for Me?	
A rich man asked Jesus what he must do to inherit life.	Rich man said he had kept all of these since his youth. Jesus said you lack one thing.	Field of Dreams
Jesus named five of the Ten Commandments and adds a new one.	Go sell all you have and give to the poor. Rich man went away sad—shocked for he was very rich.	What's the one thing that stands between us and God?
You shall not murder, commit adultery, steal, bear false witness nor defraud and honor your mother and father. Defraud is the one added.	Jesus explained to the disciples how difficult for a rich man to enter the kingdom of God.	Do we have a "what's in it for me" attitude?
They all deal with how ethically we treat one another. It involves our relationship with others.		

Pentecost 21 Year B
What's in It for Me?
Mark 10:17–31

A rich man asked Jesus what he must do to inherit eternal life. Jesus named five of the Ten Commandments: You shall not murder, You shall not commit adultery, You shall not steal, You shall not bear false witness and Honor your father and mother. He also added a new commandment: You shall not defraud. Each commandment named deals with how ethically we treat one another. They involve our relationship with others.

The rich man told Jesus he had kept these commandments since his youth but Jesus said he lacked one thing. He had to sell all he owned and give the money to the poor and follow Jesus. The rich man went away shocked as he had many possessions.

What was the rich man lacking? Was it radical discipleship? Sacrificial discipleship?

Peter asked what all the others were probably thinking, "What's in it for me?" This is called self-interest discipleship. What word describes our discipleship? What motivates us to be the hands, feet, and heart of Jesus?

In the movie, *Field of Dreams*, Ray, a farmer in Iowa, hears a voice telling him to build a baseball field instead of planting corn. Ray's livelihood depends on his corn crop, and not utilizing all of his land for crops would place the farm in arrears. But obeying the voice, Ray puts aside part of his land for a baseball field. This voice leads him step by step, and one by one he encountered Terrance Mann, a writer, a doctor who never got to bat in the major league, and of course all the baseball players who appears out of the cornfield like Shoeless Joe Jackson. All were looking for second chances. When the baseball players invited Terrance Mann to enter the cornfield with them, Ray becomes upset and asks, "What about me?" Ray states that he was the one who planted the corn under so he could build the baseball field. He was the one who had brought Terrance Mann to Iowa. He was the one who heard the voice and did what the voice said even when it didn't make any sense. All of these result in the question, what's in it for me?

All the others were getting a second chance to fulfill their dreams. When Ray thinks he is being left out, one of the baseball players asks him if he wants to play pitch. We find out this is Ray's father, and his dream of playing a game of catch with his dad would be fulfilled.

So what about us? Do we expect something in return for doing good to others and showing compassion and kindness? Are we building up brownie points with the Big Guy wanting to cash them in later? Is our discipleship radical and sacrificial where we do the crazy things the voice tells us even when it doesn't make any sense?

Jesus told the rich man he lacked one thing: Sell all his possession and give the money to the poor and he will have treasures in heaven. Jesus was asking for authentic discipleship where we have something vested. Jesus was giving him the choice to put his priorities in order and to give out of his abundance, from the center of who he was. The rich man couldn't do it.

What is our "one thing"? What is God asking us to do that we cannot allow ourselves to change our priorities and alter our life? Now is the time to step out in faith, hear the voice and obey the voice, never asking what is in it for us. In due time, we will find ourselves in a field of dreams of our own.

Pentecost 22 Year B Mark 10:35–45 Are You Able to Drink the Cup?		
James and John asked to sit on Jesus's right and left in the new kingdom. They were asking for a place of prominence, authority, and to be able to use it.	When the ten heard what James and John asked, they were angry. Jesus again tried to teach them about the greatest being a servant.	James 1:2–4 Romans 5:3–4
They had no idea what they were asking. Believed Jesus was talking about an earthly kingdom. Had not learned the greatest being last.	As followers of Christ we will encounter hardship: steep mountains, dense forests, deep oceans, and rugged paths.	Quotes from the book *Can You Drink the Cup?* by Heart Nouwen
To the right and left of Jesus at the cross were the two criminals who also were crucified. Cup and baptism represents suffering and death facing Jesus.	Through these hardships we receive greatness and learn to be servant of all.	1 Peter 5:10

Pentecost 22 Year B
Are You Able to Drink the Cup?
Mark 10:35–45

When James and John asked Jesus to let them sit on his right and left in the new kingdom, they were asking for a place of prominence, with the position on the right receiving the highest honor. They were asking to have authority and to be able to use it. They had no clue just what they were asking of Jesus, plus they still hadn't learned the lesson of the greatest being the least.

Jesus asked of them one question: "Are you able to drink the cup that I drink or be baptized with the baptism I am baptized with?" Of course they immediately replied "yes, we are able." And once again they did not understand what Jesus was asking them.

To the right and left of Jesus at the cross were the two criminals who also were to be crucified. In reality James and John were asking to be crucified with Christ. Cup and baptism are metaphors for the suffering and death Jesus faced. Jesus agreed with them that they would drink the cup and be baptized with his baptism, but only God decided who would be on the right and left.

When the ten heard what had taken place, they were angry with James and John. Jesus sees another teaching opportunity not only for James and John but all of the twelve. Jesus taught them whoever wished to be great must be a servant and the one who wished to be first must be servant of all. Jesus reminded them they came to serve, not to be served.

As followers of Christ we will each encounter hardships. There will be steep mountains, dense forests, deep oceans, and rugged paths that we will have to overcome. But it is through these hardships that we receive greatness and we learn to be servant to all.

> My brothers and sisters, whenever you face trials of any kind, consider it nothing but joy, because you know that the testing of your faith produces endurance; and let endurance have its full effect, so that you may be mature and complete, lacking in nothing.[133]
>
> And not only that, but we also boast in our sufferings, knowing that suffering produces endurance, and endurance produces character, and character produces hope, and hope does not disappoint us, because God's love has been poured into our hearts through the Holy Spirit who has been given to us.[134]

As followers of Christ, we should not look for a place where we can shine and we received all the attention and applause. We should rise each day and face our circumstances where God's will has placed us.

In the book, *Can You Drink the Cup?*, Henri Nouwen states, "We often compare our lives with those of others, trying to decide whether we are better or worse off, but such comparisons do not help us much. We have to live our life, not someone else's. We have to hold our own cup. When we are crushed like grapes, we cannot think of the wine we will become. The sorrow overwhelms us, makes us throw ourselves on the ground, face down and sweat drops of blood. Then we need to be reminded that our cup of sorrow is also our cup of joy and that one day we will be able to taste the joy as fully as we now taste the sorrow. Drinking the cup is an act of selfless love, an act

---

[133] James 1:2–4
[134] Romans 5:3–4

of immense trust, an act of surrender to a God who will give what we need when we need it."[135]

"And after you have suffered for a little while, the God of all grace, who has called you to his eternal glory in Christ, will himself restore, support, strengthen, and establish you."[136]

---

[135] *Can You Drink The Cup?* Henri Nouwen Kindle locations 149, 296, 646.
[136] 1 Peter 5:10

	Pentecost 23 Year B Mark 10:46–52 Jesus Stopped	
Synopsis of the story of Bartimaeus	Story of Bartimaeus is a lesson on how to search for, find, and develop a relationship with Christ Jesus.	Bartimaeus was poor in spirit and cried out to Jesus for mercy. Jesus stopped.
As we look closer, we see the crowd was void of compassion, therefore blind to the needs of others.	Bartimaeus heard it was Jesus	Jesus stopped for Bartimaeus and he stops for us.
"The worst calamity that could befall someone is to have eyes and fail to see" (Helen Keller).	Someone told us and we are to tell others. How else will they know?	Bartimaeus threw off his cloak and came to Jesus.
	Bartimaeus recognized Jesus as the son of David, the Messiah.	We must throw off the cloak of sin that so easily entangles and come to Jesus.
	We must study scripture so we can recognize those just claiming to be what we need and not the real deal.	Bartimaeus followed Jesus.
		We must live a lifetime following Jesus, not just momentary acts of praise.

Pentecost 23 Year B
Jesus Stopped
Mark 10:46–52

Scripture tells us a large crowd and his disciples were following Jesus to Jericho. Upon leaving, a poor blind beggar named Bartimaeus sitting by the side of the road heard that it was Jesus and cried out to him, "Jesus, Son of David, have mercy on me." Many of them tried to keep the man quiet, but Jesus stopped and called the man to him. Jesus asked Bartimaeus what he wanted Jesus to do for him. Bartimaeus wanted to see again. Jesus restored his sight and Bartimaeus became a follower.

As we look closer, we see the crowd was void of compassion and therefore blind to the needs of others. Helen Keller said, "The worst calamity that could befall someone is to have eyes but fail to see." The crowd had eyes but failed to see. Bartimaeus, though physically blind, was able to see, to perceive, to feel, to know. His spiritual sight restored his physical sight.

The story of Bartimaeus is a lesson in how to search for, find, and develop a relationship with Christ Jesus.

He heard it was Jesus, so he had to have heard the stories of all the things Jesus had done. Someone told us about Jesus and we became disciples. It is up to us to tell others about Jesus so they will seek him.

Bartimaeus recognized Jesus as the son of David, the Messiah. No one knew what the Messiah would look like, so Bartimaeus didn't need his eyes to be able to see Jesus. He had heard all the wonderful things Jesus had done and how prophecy was being fulfilled.

Bartimaeus knew in his heart that Jesus was the One. We must also study scripture so we will not be fooled by those claiming to be what we need.

Bartimaeus was poor in spirit and cried out to Jesus asked for mercy. Although the crowd tried to quiet him, he called out to Jesus even louder. Through the objections of the crowd, Bartimaeus persevered and Jesus stopped and called Bartimaeus to him just as he had called the disciples. Think about those two words: Jesus stopped. Jesus stopped for Bartimaeus and he stops for us.

Bartimaeus threw off his cloak and came to Jesus. We also must throw off the cloak of sin that so easily entangles us and come to Jesus. And like Bartimaeus, when asked what Jesus can do for us, our response should be, "Have mercy on me, Jesus, Son of David, Anointed One." Our faith should be strong enough to ask Jesus about anything and for anything, and trust if it is not best he will say no. Faith is being able to take the "no." We must be able to take the "no" even when it feels like a gut punch because our faith is strong, and we know God has a plan and it is good for our hope and future.

Bartimaeus followed Jesus. There are many unnamed healings in the Bible, but we are told this person's name, which should tell us something. It could be that Bartimaeus had a long-standing relationship with Jesus and became a well-known follower of his. His healing did not bring about momentary praise. He was in it for the long haul. We too should have staying power to follow Jesus and to praise him through the storms and the valleys.

	Pentecost 24 Year B Mark 12:28–34 How Far Are We from the Kingdom of God?	
Jesus gives Reader's Digest version of the Law: love God with all your heart, soul, mind, and strength. Love others as you love yourself.	Relationship with God	Relationship with others
First is Commandments 1–4. Second is Commandments 5–10. Love God. Love Others.	Love God with all your heart and with all your soul. Return the love God has for us into praise of him.	Love others as we love ourselves. First we love God, then ourselves and then others.
Ten Commandments are alive and well in the New Testament. Still as powerful as the ten in the Old Testament and requires obedience.	Love God with all your mind. We must communicate with God through prayer and scripture.	Kingdom of God is here and now.
	Love God with all your strength. Serving others will require the strength of faith it takes knowing the joy of the Lord is our strength.	We shouldn't be so heavenly bound that we are no earthly good.
		Love *now*.

Pentecost 24 Year B
How Far Are We from the Kingdom of God?
Mark 12:28–34

In our scripture reading today, Jesus gives us the Reader's Digest of the Law. "Hear O Israel: the Lord our God, the Lord is one; you shall love the Lord your God with all your heart, and with all your soul and with all your mind and with all your strength. You shall love your neighbor as yourself." These two commandments sums up the Ten Commandments we have in the Old Testament. The first one takes commandments one through four, which deals with our relationship with God. The second sums up commandments five through ten, which deals with our relationship with others. We might hear some people say the Ten Commandments were in the Old Testament and therefore no longer apply to us. But as you can see, they are still alive and well and require obedience in the New Testament. Just because the ten are condensed doesn't mean they do not apply to us. They are just as powerful today as they were back then. As to burnt offerings and sacrifices, they still exist but in a different form. We must sacrifice our ego and die to self and then offer ourselves to God for others.

We are to love God with all our heart and soul. Our relationship with God should be our first priority. It is the bedrock, the foundation of our living a kingdom life. The kingdom of God has come near when we return the love God has for us back into worship and praise of him.

We are to love God with all our mind. We must communicate with God through prayer and scripture. This not only requires our mind but also our hearts and souls. When we talk with (not to) God, we speak to him from the depths of our being. Deep calls to deep. When we listen, we must use our spiritual ears, our souls, and our hearts to be able to hear what God says. Sometimes our prayers change things, and other times they change us. We also must read scripture daily as God speaks through his word. We also should study the scriptures to renew our minds and for us to be transformed so we can discern the will of God. If we are not growing and learning new things about God, we will become stale, stagnate, and our lives will stink.

We are to love God with all our strength by being a servant. We face each call from the Lord with the knowledge that to please him is our strength. Most of our ministries will be difficult for us. Our ministries will change over time and new ones are added and some subtracted, but all will require us to put aside ourselves for the work for which God has assigned us. We also face each ministry knowing that God has given each of us the required gifts needed to accomplish the task and we will bear fruit.

We are to love others as we love ourselves. First we love God, then love ourselves and then love others. We cannot love ourselves without first loving God. We cannot unselfishly love others until we love ourselves and desire to do no harm to others.

Kingdom living is in the here and now. We shouldn't be so heavenly bound that we aren't any earthly good. We are to love God *now*. We are to love ourselves *now*. We are to love others *now*.

Pentecost 25 Year B
Mark 12:38–44
Putting In Our Two
Cents' Worth

Wizard of Oz Beware Dorothy Jesus says, "Beware of the Scribes."	As if on cue, a poor widow enters the treasury. He watched wealthy people put in large sums of money, but the widow put in two small coins, which was all she had.	Skin in the game. David refused land and animals. "I will not give burnt offerings to my Lord God that cost me nothing."
Scribes were teachers of the law. Some took advantage of managing widow's finances.	How do you see this woman? Social Security recipient? Single parent living on government assistance? Drug addict? Neighbor? Ourselves?	What does our discipleship cost us? What do we have that believe has little value but God can use in a big way? What is our two cents?
Jesus had called them hypocrites and brood of vipers. Knew they were guilty of false piety.	Do we give outside of self or inside of self? First fruits or what remains? Do we give of our prayers, presence, gifts, service, and our witness?	The widow gave all. Jesus gave all. We are to give all knowing Jesus will supply our every need.
	Do we give from our hearts?	

Pentecost 25 Year B
Putting In Your Two Cents' Worth
Mark 12:38–44

Remember in the *Wizard of Oz* when the Wicked Witch of the West was after Dorothy in order to get the ruby red slippers? The Wicked Witch of the West took her broom and in the sky she wrote, "Beware Dorothy." In our scripture lesson today, Jesus issued a similar warning saying, "Beware of the Scribes."

Scribes were teachers of the law, often dependent on people's gifts for their support. Some were to help manage widows' finances but often took advantage of them.[137] They strutted around in long robes wishing to be greeted with respect, have the best seats in the synagogue, and have the place of honor at banquets. They would say long prayers while devouring widows' homes. Jesus had called them hypocrites, brood of vipers, and that sums it all up. They were guilty of false piety and Jesus called them out.

As if on cue, the widow entered the treasury. Jesus watched wealthy people put in large sums of money and he watched the widow put in two small coins, all that she had to live on. In comparison, the widow gave much more than the rich people. She made the bigger sacrifice for God. We are not told her name, but we all know about her walk of faith.

We are told she was a widow, so her husband was deceased. But how do we see her? Is she an elderly woman whose only income is a Social Security check from her husband's earnings? Is she young and

---

[137] The New Interpreter's Study Bible

a single mother living off government assistance? Is she our neighbor? Is she us? The way we see this woman may reveal a lot about our own character.

Do we give outside of self or inside of self? Do we give what we have remaining or do we give from the first fruits of our labor? Do we only give money? What about our faithful participation in ministries by our prayers, our presence, our gifts, our service, and our witness? Do we give from the heart?

When King David wanted to buy land to build an altar, the landowner wanted to just give him his land and the bulls and calves for offerings. But David said, "No, I will buy them from you for a price but I will not give burnt offerings to my Lord God that cost me nothing."[138] In other words he wanted skin in the game.

What does our discipleship cost us? For some it might be money, for others it might be our time as we serve others. For some it might be the use of gifts and talents to the glory of God. What is the cost of our discipleship? What can we give or what do we have that we believe has little value but God can use in a big way? What is our two cents? Whatever it is, we are to put it all in, total surrender, knowing that when we empty ourselves, Jesus will fill us back up.

---

[138] 2 Samuel 24

About the Author

Shann Moore is a lay speaker for her district of United Methodist Churches and is often called to fill the pulpit. She was instrumental in Generative Leadership Academy in her district. She has facilitated Bible studies and Sunday school at her local church. Shann was one of the founding members of Scarlet Thread Ministries, a women's nondenominational conference group. She also has been active in Emmaus Walk and Chrysalis weekends. Shann has several previous publications in *Vista* and *Evangel* magazines.